MW01288534

Inspirational Encouraging & Heartening

# MY SOUL LOOKS BACK

Inspirational Encouraging & Heartening

# MY SOUL LOOKS BACK

*How I got Over!*

AMATUER &
PRO GOLF PLAYER
*S. Morris Holloway Jr.*

## INSPIRED BY TRUE EVENTS

*Morine S-N*

AUTHOR & MOTIVATIONAL SPEAKER

XULON PRESS

Xulon Press
2301 Lucien Way #415
Maitland, FL 32751
407.339.4217
www.xulonpress.com

© 2021 by Morine S-N

*My Soul Looks Back, How I got Over!*
*Amateur and Pro Golf Player*

All rights reserved solely by the author. The author guarantees all contents are original and do not infringe upon the legal rights of any other person or work. No part of this book may be reproduced in any form without the permission of the author. The views expressed in this book are not necessarily those of the publisher.

Due to the changing nature of the Internet, if there are any web addresses, links, or URLs included in this manuscript, these may have been altered and may no longer be accessible. The views and opinions shared in this book belong solely to the author and do not necessarily reflect those of the publisher. The publisher therefore disclaims responsibility for the views or opinions expressed within the work.

Proverbs 13:22a: A good person leaves an inheritance for their children's children, Some people's names have either been changed or remain nameless.

Unless otherwise indicated, Scripture quotations taken from the Holy Bible, New International Version (NIV). Copyright © 1973, 1978, 1984, 2011 by Biblica, Inc.™. Used by permission. All rights reserved.

Printed in the United States of America

Paperback ISBN-13: 978-1-6628-0628-5
Dust Jacket ISBN-13: 978-1-6628-0629-2
Ebook ISBN-13: 978-1-6628-0630-8

Illustrations by Juztin Helms

and

K'lyn Brown

# DEDICATED

To my dad,

Square Morris Holloway Jr.

# CONTENTS

# ACKNOWLEDGMENTS

M rs. Hazel Carter and Mr. Carter were instrumental in my life. They made a difference in my transition from Alabama to Ohio. Mother Carter took me under her wings and adopted me into their family when I first arrived in Springfield. I didn't have any relatives in Springfield, but she always treated me like one of her sons. Mr. Carter introduced me to golf circles and members of an all-black golf club after I had become established in Springfield, Ohio, which opened quite a few doors for me. I owed a lot of my success at the game of golf to Mr. Carter who taught me how to be competitive.

Edith Cassidy, the chief technician at Mercy Hospital, was instrumental in my success as a lab technician. She had a lot of confidence in me. She assigned me to the night technician role at Mercy Hospital. Dr. Mary P. Hunter, the pathologist, approved of this appointment. This was a prestigious position. I was responsible for running the lab all by myself. Being allowed to do this laid the foundation for other successes in my career as a lab technician and played a significant part in what was to come.

Thanks to my mother, Chanie Holloway, I was able to persevere through hard knocks in life. She sent up her prayers for me and all of her children for many years. I know it was the grace of God that allowed me the successes that I experienced in life.

I thank those who continued to fight against social injustices for all people throughout the years, in ways that some of us could not. Many paved the way for Blacks in our society as well as in *the sport of golf.*

*Thank you to everyone that contributed to the production of this book; Victor-Epistat-E-Consulting and The Production Team at Xulon Press.*

# FATHER'S DAY

M y daughters came to my house on Father's Day, and we celebrated it by spending the entire day together. We began conversing about my past experiences and how it felt being an African American raised in the South during the 1940s through the 1960s. I told them different stories about how it was to grow up in Birmingham, Alabama, and about some of my life experiences. We had a good time that day. I think that day opened up a lot more memories about my childhood and different things that I had been through in life. Later that day, I sat back in my recliner chair, and my soul looked back and began to think about *how it was that I got over.*

For centuries, African Americans have had to face challenges and obstacles if for no other reason than the color of their skin. Some of those obstacles came not only from other races, but some of those challenges caused us to have to stand against the opposition within our own race as well.

Our nation as a whole has had to overcome tenacious challenges against racism due to opinions constructed by men. There were lines drawn that brought about the American Civil War that then led to the Emancipation Proclamation and the Civil Rights movement. There were lines drawn in this country that called upon heroic people to take a stand—people like Rosa Parks, a woman arrested because she wouldn't give up her seat to a white man on the bus when he couldn't find a seat in the white section. There were also people like the nine black students, known as the Little Rock Nine, who arrived at Central High School to attend a previously all-white High School or people like the four college students who took a stand against segregation in Greensboro, North Carolina, by refusing to leave Woolworth's lunch counter without being served. Then there were people, like the seven black and six white activists known as The "Freedom Ride," who rode the Greyhound bus, touring through the segregated southern parts of America, to protest segregated bus terminals. Some people stood up to housing discrimination based on their race, sex, national origin, and religion.

Blacks stood in lines for hours to take a literacy test just to be given the right to vote. There were people like John Lewis who led the March of Washington demonstration known as "Bloody Sunday," and the many others who marched alongside him. They dedicated their lives to ending segregation and to assisting blacks with voter registration. Great people like Martin Luther King Jr. , the minister, and leader in the civil rights movement, played a tremendous part in the success of ending legal segregation in the southern parts of the United States.

It was during this era that the Jim Crow laws were being enforced to maintain racial segregation in the southern United States. Jim Crow laws kept Blacks from having access to the same justice and opportunities as white people. Among many other injustices, they also denied Blacks the right to play sports against any white person. This meant that black golfers were denied the right to compete against white golfers on the green. They were also denied the opportunities they had earned in this sport and were looked upon as less than their white competitors. Despite the obstacles many encountered, they continued to flourish and succeed in their game.

Ted Rhodes and Bill Spiller fought the PGA against their Caucasian-only clause for years. In the 1948 US Open, Theodore "Ted" Rhodes was acknowledged as the first African American professional golfer John Shippen played in the second US Open at Shinnecock Hills, where he had once worked as a caddie, at the age of seventeen years. Pete Brown became the first African American player to win a PGA-sanctioned event and the Waco Turner Open. Lee Elder was the first African American to play in the Masters and won four times on the PGA Tour and eight times on the Champions Tour. Charlie Sifford filed a lawsuit against the PGA for not being able to enter into the PGA golf tour. Eventually, the courts ruled in his favor and allowed him to play, removing the (PGA's) "Caucasian-only clause." He became the first prominent black player able to play professional PGA. He opened the proverbial gate for black golfers. There were other great golf players like Calvin Peete, James Black, Nathaniel Stark, and Joe Roach, who all made their mark in the sport of golf and broke through the barriers set before them.

I was among those black amateur and pro golf players of that era, and I also faced some of the same challenges as my predecessors. My name is Square Morris Holloway Jr., and I was able to overcome the barriers put up by both the white and black cultures of my time. I did not consider myself to be the best golfer, yet I was noted for being a young black man who pursued his dreams despite the odds. In stubborn perseverance to succeed in life, I crossed lines that were construed by people. *My Soul Looks Back: How I got Over!* shares my stories and my experiences.

# PART I

## CHILDHOOD TO MANHOOD

A labama *is known, historically, as one of the largest slaveholding states for African Americans in the United States. As a result of the free labor and the prosperous cotton trade, contributed to by slavery, Alabama became one of the wealthiest ten states of the Union.*

*In 1861, the American Civil War began between the United States of America and the Confederate States of America. The Confederate States consisted of eleven southern states that left the Union in 1860 and 1861 in disagreement over the legalism of slavery. On April 9, 1865, General Robert E. Lee and his Confederate troops surrendered to the United States of America, putting an end to the four-year American Civil War. Lincoln signed the Emancipation Proclamation that freed all Blacks enslaved in the Confederate States, and a decade of reconstruction began. With the Confederate States' defeat and the announcement that all slaves were now declared legally free from slavery, Alabama could no longer depend on the free labor that it had once benefitted from. As a result, Alabama suffered economic losses and hardship. Most of the farmers no longer owned their own land. Some had to become sharecroppers and laborers themselves. Alabama slowly transitioned into a poor rural state.*

*Even though freedom for Blacks had been legally declared throughout the country, many white people continued to treat African American people as second-class citizens. African Americans experienced such inequities as segregation, which contributed to black people being treated with cruelty and brutality, underfunded black schools, black lynchings, and other injustices. This treatment was far worse for black people residing in the southern states, where Jim Crow Laws furthered racial segregation.*

# From My Window

From my window I see

Beautiful yellow and red leaves

Falling from the trees.

The flowers are parched

From the long summer's sun.

They are covered with webs

Which spiders have spun.

— S. Morris Holloway

# Chapter 1

# LIFE IN THE SOUTH

I was born on July 11, 1944, in Birmingham, Alabama, the firstborn son of Square Morris Sr. and Chanie Holloway. As the oldest son, I was respectfully given the title of Square Morris Holloway Jr. I know the name Square might seem a little strange to some, but as different as the name is, it's held its many advantages over the years.

My mother was born in Red Fox Kentucky, and she was the third of nine children. My father and mother met in Hazard, Kentucky, when they first started dating. My mother was twenty-one years old, and my father was in his forties when they married and moved to Birmingham, Alabama, in 1940. The older men in the family used to joke around with my dad and tease him because of how much younger my mother was than him, telling him he was "robbing the cradle." And truthfully, he was, but they were happy together. Sure, they had their times when they were up as well as those times when they were down just like any married couple does. But for the most part, they got along well and were good to one another.

My mother was a very religious and meticulous woman. She was brown-skinned and a fairly attractive-looking black woman who stood about 5 feet, 5 inches tall and had a pretty nice build. Once she and daddy married, she became a homemaker, better known today as a stay-at-home mom. She was still pretty young when she started bearing children. As a young adult, she had the responsibility of taking care of the home, us kids, and my father, while he worked and made the money.

My father was an entrepreneur. Because he was a business owner, he was considered a big timer in our community. He never knew it then, but he was a man before his time. It was unusual for a black person to be an entrepreneur. Most black people were known for working at either the city's steel mills in the local area called Rocchetta and blast furnaces. My father carried a professional demeanor around with him everywhere he went. He was a bit stout with very broad shoulders. He was brown-skinned in complexion and kept his hair cut fairly short. He was a clean-cut man. A real sharp dresser, he would be dressed in business attire on most occasions when you saw him. I mean, he was dressed "to the T." It was said that he dressed very well for a man who lived and grew up in Grove Hill, Alabama. Women back then loved a nicely dressed black man.

The population in Alabama back then, in total, was about 2,800,900. The black population was around 980,000. At that time, Blacks living in the state of Alabama underwent many disadvantages which came in many forms. They were sometimes faced with violence, as well as limitations placed by segregation, inadequate school funding, voter disqualification, and many other injustices. Our family lived in a small community in the city of Birmingham called Cape Town, where everybody knew everybody. If you were seen doing something that you should not have been doing, it was sure to get back to one of your parents. This was good in that it helped to keep a lot of us in line growing up at that time.

There were eight of us children all together in our household. Large black families were common back then. The people in the town said every time they looked up it seemed like my momma was pregnant. She had some of us back to back, and every one of her children was born at home. Babies back then were normally born at home. They called them home births.

Dr. Drake helped deliver all eight of us children. Dr. Drake was a prominent black doctor in the community of Fairfield, Alabama. He was a high-class doctor and smoked cigars. He was a man who knew who he was and was proud of who he was as a black professional, and you could see it in his walk, his talk, and how he carried himself. He was a very small man, short in stature, yet he was intimidated by none, even though he couldn't have weighed more than a "buck 0 five," Which means he didn't weigh much at all.

Every time Dr. Drake came around, we found out that Momma was pregnant. So it got to the point that every time we saw him in the house, we knew we would soon have another sister or brother. When my younger brother Freddie was born, it was a very upsetting turn for the family. Freddie was a twin. He came out fine and was very healthy, but the other twin, named Eddie, died. That was a very sad day in our home. I still recall the grief upon my mother's face. It was an unforced atmosphere of mourning that was prevalent throughout the house.

Dr. Drake and my dad were two of the few black male role models for us young black boys. They were both positive role models. Unfortunately, that was not as easy to find as it probably should have been. And then one day, Dr. Drake was here and what seemed like the next day, he was gone because in a home invasion, someone broke into his home, tied him up, tortured him, and killed him. They later discovered his dead body in his home. He had been in there, dead for some time.

A lot of people were upset about his death. The worst part was that they never found out who did it. It became one of those unsolved cases, or so they said. Though nobody knew who did it, we all had our suspicions, Back then it was not unusual for Whites to get away with killing a black person. And most of the time, the killings were done for no significant reasons at all. Just being black was enough reason.

Though we never witnessed any lynchings or brutal beatings up close and personal, we were well aware of the difference in our skin color—that of being black versus being white. We had also heard the stories of different incidents through friends and people talking in the neighborhood. My mother sheltered us and tried to keep a tight grip on all of her children. The sheltering was an effort to try to protect us from the horrifying images of the violence that came along with the racial injustices against Blacks as well as to prevent us from becoming one of those statistics ourselves.

We had a pretty good family unit growing up. There were many other families about our size, who were raised during that time and era that did not have it as well as we did. Even though we had our share of hard times and struggles, overall, I would say we were one of the more fortunate ones. Our house was a block up from the community grade school, Gary Ensley. About five miles from Gary Ensley was the community middle school, Edgewater. A little bit further up the road and to the left of Edgewater School was one of several high schools, Westfield High. Each one of us children attended and graduated from all three of these schools. Like I said, "I lived in a rather small town."

We lived next door to Mr. Elliot and his family. Mr. Elliot's wife went by the name of Miss Jimmy, and they had one daughter named Penny. Mr. Elliot was well known throughout the community. The people in the community gave him the nickname "the old-timer." We called him "the old-timer" because he held onto his old-school life-style, even though the world gradually changed around him. By our community's standards, he was rather eccentric. Many days, we would see Mr. Elliot set high in his wagon that was pulled by his mule, old Bell, wearing his overalls and wide brim hat. He didn't own an automobile, and Bell was his sole source of transportation throughout the neighborhood and short excursions, in and out of town, to Wylam. He employed Bell to plow home gardens for households in the neighborhood, charging his customers a small fee. He raised chickens and had some hogs that he kept on his modest-sized homesite next to old Bell's corral.

Our house was built on the red dirt fields on the outskirts of Birmingham. It was a nice house, built on a nice piece of land with many other very nice Black-owned homes. We had four bedrooms and one bathroom that was located right next to the master bedroom. There were three bedrooms in the back of the house and one in the front, right behind our kitchen. There was a porch on the front side of the house where we spent a lot of time, especially when it was really hot, which was often. The porch was parallel to my dad's store that was attached to the house.

The house had two living rooms, a dining room, and an unfinished room along the back end of the house. I do recall there being lots and lots of rooms in this house. This worked out in our family's favor since we had a house full of children. There were ten of us in total including my mom and dad. So, you see, even though our home was pretty big, it felt rather small when we all came together. But we were very fortunate. The most important part of our house was my father's grocery store. Let me tell you, it was grand!

My dad was really proud of that store. There was a sign that read, "Holloway Grocery," on full display out front. There was a big window right in the front of the store where Dad displayed all of his fruit. I remember seeing the most perfect, unblemished fruits on display, filling up one of my mother's fancy bowls. There were bowls full of all types of fruits such as bananas, oranges, apples, peaches, plums, and many other tasty fruits. The store had a lot of shelves, and they were all filled with lots and lots of canned goods of different sorts. He even had some shelves full of some of the best meats a black family could buy.

On the counter were four jars of freshly baked cookies that sat on top of a glass-enclosed case. Inside the glass case, Dad kept the penny candy as well as the nickel and dime assorted candy bars. There was a refrigerator behind the counter that stayed full of BB bottling company soda pops. Next to that was the freezer where he kept ice cream items such as popsicles, ice cream, and ice cream bars. You name it, he had it. My dad's philosophy was that pennies make nickels, nickels make dimes, and dimes eventually make dollars.

And if that wasn't enough to catch your eye, right in front of the store were two gas pumps. Yes, I said "gas pumps!" This was the first grocery store gas station that I had ever heard of at that time. If you were to set your eyes upon that grocery store today, you would have still been impressed. My dad was a semi-genius if I were to say so myself. You'll see later on why I called him a semi-genius.

The people in Cape Town thought that my father was rich because he owned a grocery store. In a way, he was rich but not in the way that many people in the community defined being rich. His richness was not built on his monetary value, but he was rich with ideas and possibilities. Yet, my dad was able to make a comfortable living from the store. We were much better off than some of the other families in our neighborhood, and we were able to enjoy some of the luxuries that many other families were unable to.

Despite Dad's success, he was a very modest man, never looking down on anyone. He catered to all the Blacks in the community. He extended lines of credit to many of the people in the neighborhood, who shopped from his store. And they would faithfully come into the store at the end of the month and settle their accounts.

I remember when my dad bought the family our first TV set. This was a luxury that many black families were unable to afford. We were the first black family in the neighborhood to get a TV set and the first to have an indoor bathroom installed in our home. In spite of all we had from my dad's good fortune, he was always willing to share with others. He never thought that it could ever come back to bite him in the behind like a snake. Back then, when black people started to see other Blacks getting ahead, it normally caused a sense of jealousy.

I still remember our living room being filled with the neighbors on many occasions. My dad invited them over to watch TV on special occasions, such as the big Joe Louis World championship fights or the World Series matches. Of course, he charged them 5 to 10 cents each to enter. He never could let go of his entrepreneurial bent. I imagine when he went to bed, instead of counting sheep, he was counting the till at the grocery store.

Success was not something that came easy for my father. Just like any other successful businessman, he had to work hard to bring his vision to fruition. He was a hard and faithful worker, working tirelessly to maintain the store during the day and driving a private taxicab, the Jitney Cab Service, by night. As hard as he worked, I think there were times when I don't think he saw it as work at all but more like his mission. The people in our town were fine with my dad's success for a while. Over time, my dad's grocery stores began making a substantial profit. And that was fine with black folks until he began to spend some of that well-earned money. Once black folks could see his prosperity up close, then they began to have a problem with his success.

One day, much to our surprise, my father came home with a forest green secondhand Cadillac he had bought. My dad looked like a boy in a candy store when he looked at that Cadillac. Though it was a used Cadillac, it was grand. It had all the fancy fixtures like an AM and FM radio with an automatic transmission and power brakes. My dad was so proud of this car. Just about as much as he was of his store.

As time went on, Mom said she began to hear that people around town were talking about Daddy, saying that he was getting too big for his britches and had forgotten where he came from. The truth was that some of Dad's so-called friends and neighbors had gotten jealous of his success. Gradually, my dad began losing customers. At first, it was a small few who stopped coming to the store, and then he noticed he wasn't seeing his regular customers as much. We found out later that people began shopping over at Revere's Market This was a White-owned Jewish grocery store, located several miles away in a small community known as Wylam.

They refused to continue to shop at my Dad's store anymore. They said they were not going to allow Holloway to get rich off their backs. It didn't happen overnight, but soon my dad's store was no longer profitable, and eventually, he had to close his doors for good. I can still remember my dad's face on the last day when he shut the store's doors. It was as if twenty years had been stripped from his life that day, and they would never return. I have never forgotten that look on my father's face, and I have carried that experience with me all of my life.

After that, our family fell on some pretty hard times financially. One day, while playing the dozens with my friends, one of the boys made the joke saying that old man Holloway had gone from "sugar to S***." This was a joke that some jealous people in the community had come up with to hurt my dad. Hearing those words upset me. I gained my composure and fired back by making a joke about his mother swallowing a giant watermelon seed. I knew this would hurt him because his mother had a big belly due to a tumor she had in her stomach. This was a low blow, but he never knew how deep his comment had hurt me. The truth is, it cut to the core of my very soul. This was my father's tornado that had also become his children's tornado. I never forgot how people, who I thought should have been supporting us, became a hindrance to their own people's success. I was determined that I would never let my own people tear me down again.

# Chapter 2
# TORNADO

## Birmingham Alabama, Tornado of 1956

O ur family was to face many challenges over the years. Some of these challenges would also be filled with emotional pain. Like the challenge that not only we, but our entire city faced as a result of the tornado that hit Birmingham, Alabama, in 1956. This was a tornado that moved the hearts and souls of our town to the most memorable sorrows. They say that natural tornadoes can occur any time of the year. Who would have known that this one particular day would be that time? Our family had just returned home from church, and I headed right outside in the back and started practicing my golf swing.

I should have known there was just something about that day; I could feel it in the air. The wind tossed and turned like it was in a restless sleep. The leaves gave off a whistle as the leaves danced to the tune of the wind. If only we could do the things that we see trees do. If only we could be so limber and bend the way they do and be so resilient to the opposition. It so amazes me to see the limbs on a tree bend so easily and so easily alter their shape in response to the wind.

Most boys my age were into different things. They were playing sports like football or basketball. But the game for me was golf. This was all that I thought about most of my days. Some people are self-made; I was self-taught. I had it in my mind that if I was going to play golf, I was going to be the best at it, and that's what I set out to do. The sun was beaming down fearlessly, and I was surely feeling its effects. With each swing of my club, my face dripped beads of sweat that steadily and slowly rolled down my face. My shirt was almost completely soaked in perspiration, mixed with a lot of determination.

I was determined to master my swinging technique. Golf had not only become a favorite sport of mine, but it was my passion. The quest for perfection kept me pushing and pushing to do more with my swing every time I gripped a club. I worked toward developing consistency in my swing. Of course, the advantage of a consistent swing did not show up until much later in life. Sometimes I felt like when that ball swiveled its way into the air, I was right alongside it. I would watch it disappear online and into the sky. It was as if I was touching the clouds as well.

Alongside that ball, I could fly beyond the challenges that I was destined to face as a black man living in that society despite the challenges of the known and unknown. It was only later in life that I found out that I could face new challenges. It was only as a grown man that I realized the only real limitations that we have are the ones that we have created from within. Though the challenges were there, the determination to rise above and to exceed those limitations were greater. According to the Bible, "As a man thinketh in his heart, so is he" (Proverbs 23:7).

After a few swings, I noticed trickles of rain and dashes of light that began dancing across the sky. What started as just a light rain quickly transitioned into something much more; I didn't have a chance to prepare for what was to happen next. Before I knew it, the wind began blowing even harder. The vines along the fence were being torn off by the mere passing of what was once a gentle wind. When I looked in the sky, I saw the once blue-green sky as it went completely black. I knew then something was on the way, and I quickly made a dash for the back door.

Unfortunately, it was not quick enough. I know in reality I was moving much faster than this, but as I was running it felt like my body was moving in slow motion. My body was fighting the wind to continue forward. Mounds of dirt gushed across the yard. All I could see was red dirt blocking my vision. I covered my eyes with my hands while still trying to keep sight of my house. As I covered my face with my hands, I could see neighbors running about, trying to make it into their homes in every direction as well.

I'm not sure how long it took me to get to the door. It could have been only seconds, but it seemed like a lifetime at that moment. I recall looking back into the sky and seeing just barely within a distance a funnel in the cloud. It reminded me of a freight train running rapidly up the railroad. I later found out that my dad was right up the street. He too had seen the tornado as it was approaching and jumped into a nearby ditch to escape its destruction.

As I made it into the house, it took me a while to calm down and catch my breath. My hands wouldn't stop shaking. I remember my mother gathering all the siblings together in the kitchen and praying. She prayed loud and long, passing over each of us and anointing our heads with oil. First, she anointed me, then my oldest sister La Grieta, my sister Sherry, and then my sisters Delotha and Marcia, and my brothers Freddie and Reginald. There all eight of us were crouched down on the kitchen floor covering our heads with our hands as Mother hovered over us that day. I closed my eyes, and I think that I prayed the hardest I had ever prayed before in my life at that age. Momma stood there in the kitchen praying. She said, "Hush, God is doing His work!"

I don't know if it was all in my head or I heard the sounds of people screaming. It could have been the screams that were coming from within me. The noises simultaneously grew louder, making it impossible to hear a particular sound because the sound was so deafeningly loud. We heard as the winds blew through trees and sounds of buildings being torn apart and the hail and torrential rain that beat upon the roof. Suddenly it all gave way to a dead calm, followed by intense wind. The loud sounds of sirens could be heard across the field toward Stacy Hollow. As Momma prayed, the storm soon passed. After the tornado passed, the neighbors all came out to check their properties for damage. Fortunately, the tornado did not hit our neighborhood as badly as it had hit the community of Stacy Hollow.

I went back outside and finished off where I had left, swinging my golf clubs. After hitting a few balls, I decided to walk toward Stacy

Hollow, only to find the road blocked off. I knew another passageway off the highway. This was a shortcut through a wooded area that some of the kids discovered. It was then that I was able to see the extensive damage that the tornado had caused. There were dead chickens, hogs, and livestock all across the road. Some houses had been knocked down to their foundations with nothing left at all but debris. It looked as if an atomic bomb had hit the community. I had no idea that the tornado had destroyed some of Stacy Hollow. They said Birmingham was in the middle of Tornado Alley that day. I later found out that one of my classmates had been killed and another had lost her leg.

The craziness of it all was, the Friday before the tornado hit, one of the missionaries in my mother's church had been out on the street corner preaching that God was going to bring some destruction upon the community of Stacy Hollow because of the people's sinfulness. Stacy Hollow had a lot of what we called "rough dudes." Ironically, the missionary's house had not been touched by the tornado. Not even a shingle was missing from her roof. This was a true miracle. We realized this after looking upon the devastation surrounding this area.

Many people lost a lot of things that were valuable to them that day; some even lost their lives. It was a tornado that we would never forget. Returning to school, we were informed that three or four of our classmates had lost family members as a result of this tornado. At least twenty people all together within the community had been killed. This pulsated in the minds of our people for years to come. For some time after that, whenever the sky began to get cloudy, some students would freak out. It would be the start of a cry in remembrance of the tragedy that took place on this day. It taught us to cherish the lives that we had and to cherish the lives God had given us and our loved ones. For we never know when God will call our number, and our time on the earth will be but a memory.

# Chapter 3
# THE CADDY CALL

*Hard Times*

My dad's store closure had a major impact on our family financially as well as emotionally. As with any family that experiences a financial loss or hardship, it tends to cause some disharmony in the home. My mother and father seemed to argue more than usual, over things like money, the kids, and most of all, religion. Things got heated when Momma joined a Pentecostal church. This was a problem because my dad was a diehard member of the Baptist church.

The Pentecostal and Baptist churches were different from each other in many ways. The Pentecostal church was a sanctified church or Holy Ghost–filled church. The Pentecostals were a lot stricter; they had a lot of rules that the members had to adhere to, such as modest dress among women and hair guidelines for men and women. They didn't believe in women wearing makeup, jewelry, or pants. Some were even forbidden to go to movies or attend sports events. They were what many might call legalistic. They tarried for the Holy Ghost by calling on the name of Jesus and believed the evidence of someone being filled with the Holy Ghost was when they spoke in tongues.

They both also worshipped differently. Pentecostals allowed dancing, shouting, and praying out loud during worship services. Their praise was a lot more elaborate than the Baptists. They believed in lively worship. It was not considered worship if there wasn't any praying out loud, clapping hands, shouting, and banging on some tambourines. In many Pentecostal churches, the women were allowed to serve as preachers, missionaries, and in some cases, pastors. They also ordained women and or even placed them in roles to lead congregations.

The Baptist church that Daddy attended was sedate. Their atmosphere was a lot more laid back than the Pentecostals. They didn't think it took a lot to get saved, be saved, and stay saved. Once you confessed and said you were saved, then *you were saved*. For Daddy, it was that simple. You could praise God in many ways, and you didn't have to wake the neighborhood to do it. Daddy, along with many of the other Baptists, believed that the only people who went to the Pentecostal church were low, downtrodden people.

When Momma left the Baptist church and went to the Pentecostal church, Daddy was extremely upset. We would hear them argue over this on many nights. We didn't know when peace would come over this situation. But it was just as Mom always said, "This too shall pass," and eventually it did. Over the years the Pentecostal church began to make a lot of transitions from within. They began promoting education more. Step-by-step, that so-called downtrodden religion became a more respected religion that attracted more prosperous and influential people. People with career occupations, such as doctors, lawyers, and other professional careers, began joining the church.

Years later, Momma became an ordained pastor and started a church in the community of Mulga, Alabama. Of course, this was not a shock to her children or anybody who knew our mother. Most of our memories of Momma throughout our childhood was of her being in church. At night, Momma was at church. Daytime, she was at church; the church became Momma's second home. Every time she went to church, she dragged her children with her. I told myself that when I became an adult, I was not going to step foot into a church again. I mean really what for? Back then, the way that I looked at it, I didn't need to go to church ever again. My church account was in overflow. Of course, later in life as an adult, I eventually got over that.

## *Mountain Brook*

Over time, our family's financial situation continued to decline, and it eventually got to the point where Dad could no longer afford to provide certain provisions as he had before. The older children in the family helped out by getting jobs and purchasing their own school clothes. That was what led me to Mr. Charlie Hunter. Charlie was a slick-and-sly, fast-talking, I-got-what-you-need, wannabe businessman. He was also one of the best caddy masters in the city of Birmingham, Alabama, and a godsend to our community. Charlie was a heavyset black man who always wore a white shirt, pants, and a white outer jacket that always appeared to be too tight and sloppily worn, showing his potbelly peeking from under his shirt with his every move.

With each breath, he made a noticeable wheezing sound. That sound normally followed a prolonged cough that would probably work your nerves after some time spent in his company. No one was sure what old Charlie was suffering from. It could have been COPD or emphysema, a breathing condition that heavy smokers get. He smoked Camel cigarettes and drank Seagram's gin. As Charlie would say, "Drink gin! It ain't no sin!" He also had a habit of stopping by the state store every day after leaving the golf course to make sure he kept some gin in stock. Good old Charlie! Charlie cussed like a sailor and drank like one too.

Regardless of his demeanor, Charlie was a man with certain connections. To do what Charlie was doing, you had to have a white social network. Charlie introduced me and many other young boys to a world we never knew existed. This was the unique world of the Mountain Brook community located above downtown Birmingham, Alabama. Mountain Brook was formally called Mountain Brook City. It arose from the Mountain Brook Estates community that was developed in the 1920s. This community was built with the idea that the future residents would be white, wealthy Birmingham business leaders.

The community was restricted to Whites only, and it only allowed a few types of businesses to move into the community. Due to the lack of access into the community, many of the residents had automobiles for transportation. This area consisted of restricted paved roads for automobile travel to keep as much of the public out as possible. These Mountain Brook residents became known as "brookies" by the people in Birmingham. We saw them as white people living in lavish homes and having luxurious lifestyles. This was a life unique to the lifestyle of the people living in the city of Birmingham. Mountain Brook was praised for its mansions and its spectacular landscaped yards and best-kept homesites that we had ever seen. It was in Mountain Brook that the high-class segregated country clubs were found, such as the private Birmingham Country Club, Vestavia Country Club, and Mountain Brook Club. These clubs provided golf, swimming, tennis, and other exclusive social activities for their members.

The Mountain Brook Country Club was where Charlie would teach us to caddy. Or as Charlie would say, "make some money!" We called these trips to the Country Club "going to the mountain." We didn't understand at that time that we were literally "going up to the mountain." Once we arrived in the Mountain Brook community, we were astonished by the view of their plush residential homes with well-manicured lawns and shaped shrubbery. Our faces were mesmerized as we passed by these homes where the residents' land was being tended to by the residents as well as their gardeners. I never knew people could live that way. By living that way, I mean "prosperous."

This showed me a life full of possibilities and a life full of things I had never seen before. Seeing this helped me to understand why Blacks worked for these white business owners. The pay was good, and we got a glimpse into their daily lifestyles. In time, a bus service was established from downtown Birmingham to Mountain Brook. Blacks were then provided easy transportation to the domestic jobs readily available "on the mountain."

Charlie drove a black 1952 Chevy car. He loaded all of us boys, ages twelve and up, himself, and his wife, Muda, into it. He and Muda would be in the front seats and about six or seven boys squeezed into the back seat. We were packed in that car like a can of sardines. That was before the seat belt laws. We would get stares as we passed other vehicles. This drew a chuckle from the local police as well, as Charlie drove by with his crew. This never bothered Charlie because this was his business.

Charlie's wife, Muda was a tall black woman about six feet tall. She was brown-skinned and shapely and had profoundly large buttocks. We sometimes made fun of her butt for being large enough to put a saddle on. Muda was very loyal to Charlie, and she would assist him in any way that she could with his small entrepreneurial hustle. She was also the only one who had any influence or control over Charlie. When he was upset, she had to step in on several occasions and calm him down.

Charlie was always prepared for these trips to Mountain Brook. Charlie and Muda brought up bin loads of whiting fish and pork chops. Of course, some of this fish had expired and possessed a strong foul smell. Charlie would sometimes allow us caddies to earn some extra perks by cleaning the whiting fish for Muda. Charlie and his wife Muda would set up a food service at the caddy shack. The caddy shack was a building for the caddies to hang out in-between their caddying. It was right across from this lavish building known as the Mountain Brook Country Club. It had two rooms and a bathroom that was always too filthy to use. Most of the caddies resorted to using the "facilities," a wooded area out in the back of the shack, if you know what I mean.

Muda provided fish and pork chop sandwiches at the shack and served them up to us caddies. They knew that after caddying all day, the caddy would eventually get hungry. You could smell the aroma of Muda's fish and pork chops clear back to Cape Town. She made some of the best whiting fish and pork chop sandwiches that you could ever get in the State of Alabama. We nicknamed the whiting fish "whale tails."

Charlie kept what he called a money-pay-back book. Every time we looked up, he had it in his hands and was writing something in it. It was in this book that Charlie kept the numbers of the cash that each caddy owed him. Each caddy was given a cash voucher after caddying, and Charlie would cash in these vouchers at the end of the day and deduct the caddy's tab from what they had earned that day.

21

The caddy's tab started from the time that we stepped into his vehicle clear to the time that we stepped out. Charlie charged us for the ride up to Mountain Brook, and he charged us for the ride back. He charged us for the food and anything else that he could think of to charge us for. As the need grew, so did his list. If you had a need, he had the answer. But you could be sure it came with a cost. That was how Charlie operated. It was a known fact that late in the evening after the Mountain Brook Club had closed, Charlie could be seen walking from the club to the Caddy Shack with his cash box under his arms, his potbelly peeking from under his shirt, in a slow tuckered-out walk.

The Mountain Brook Clubhouse was a fairly large club with a few hundred, white, well-endowed members. These members included prosperous people, such as industrialists, bankers, realtors, and other businessmen. The club had a golf pro shop near the front of the building and a golf course off to the right side of the club. The only Blacks allowed in the club were those who worked in the club. Charlie was allowed to go in as far as the pro shop. He was what many people called an Uncle Tom at the time, and he had no problem with this. When he addressed the white men at the Club, it was always with "Yes sir, boss man," "No sir, boss man," "Let me get that for you sir, boss man" or "How can I help you sir, boss man." He was all but only a little short of saying "Yes a master, sir, boss man." He would later laugh about it with the caddies about how he used his Uncle Tom savvy to hustle the white man out of his money.

Uncle Tom or not, Charlie Hunter was serious about his caddying and made sure that we were well prepared. He taught us caddies the basics of becoming "good caddies." He emphasized that if you hear the outcry "fore" that it meant we were to duck down! An errant golf ball was heading your way. Our job was to carry the bag and watch the golf balls for the golfers. This was an important part of our task since a lost ball meant penalty strokes added to the golfer's score. Another important task for us caddies on the green was to hold the flag and pull the flag from the hole as instructed by the golfer.

We enjoyed the trip up about as much as we did get to caddy. There was never a dull moment with Charlie. Charlie was as crazy and crooked as he was a jokester. He always had a lot of fun with us cad-dies. He had nicknames for all of us, like Jack Jones, Funny Shape, Big Face, Hook, and Spanky, just to name a few. There was never a dull moment in his presence. He always found some sort of way to make fun of somebody in the group.

When the golfers were ready for a caddy, Charlie lined up the golf bags in a row in front of the club. Then Charlie went down the list, calling out caddies' names. Sometimes we had a single bag, and some-times we had a double bag. It was always important to be attentive if Charlie was calling your name. If your name was called, you went on to caddy. If your name wasn't called to caddy, you didn't caddy, which meant you didn't make any money. It was that simple. On very rare occasions, there were not enough golfers to hire a caddy. Charlie knew if a caddy did not make money, then he didn't get the money they owed him for the food they ate and the transportation he provided to and from the golf course.

It went like this. "Fat Head!" he shouted out. Once our name was called, you would step up, grab the bag, and you went down to the first tee area, awaiting the golfers to come out of the clubhouse and claim their bag and caddy. Sometimes the golfer would decide to hit some practice balls into a designated area and have the caddy collect those balls. The caddy could also earn an extra fee for "shagging" or picking up these practice balls.

Even though Charlie liked having fun, he had rules for his cad-dies, and no fighting was one of them. One day, a few of these caddies decided to do a little gambling in their spare time, and an argument broke out. Jack Jones was one of the ones arguing. He was a snaggle-tooth roughneck who nobody messed with. When the argument broke out between him and another caddy, he went out in the woods, grabbed a branch the size of a log, and knocked the other dude upside the head. Bam! That guy hit the ground like a sack of rocks. There was blood everywhere, and I do mean everywhere. Eventually, the other guy stumbled up onto his feet and tried to save face, but by that time he was way too late and way too short of a dollar. The guy swore he was going to kill Jack Hunter. When Jack heard him say that, he went back after him. Had Charlie not intervened, that guy might have been a thing of the past that day.

It was a known fact to everybody that Charlie was the head n****r in charge and what he said went. If he didn't say it, then it didn't mean anything. You had to be plum crazy to try Charlie, but some gave it a go. One day in mind was during a caddy call. One of the caddies took one of the bags without Charlie's permission and went down to the first tee. This was an older guy. When Charlie found out what he had done, he took the boy that he had assigned the caddy down to the tee area and took the bag away from the other guy.

As Charlie started back up the hill to the front of the club, the guy followed Charlie and started cursing at him, then kicked Charlie in the butt. Why he did that, only God knows. Charlie headed straight for the caddy shack. He huffed and puffed his way up that hill like a bat out of hell. As fast as he started, he slowed down, being distracted by his persistent cough. His run quickly turned into a very slow walk, yet he made it to the caddy shack. We all knew that Charlie kept a pistol hidden somewhere in the caddy shack. When the other guy realized where Charlie was going, he turned around and got out of dodge, fast! Two white officers arrived sometime after that with the guy in hand. Charlie said, "That's him, boss man, arrest his a**." The cops just laughed and took the guy away. We suspected that they probably let him go later since no charges were filed.

During our time with good old Charlie, we learned a whole lot more than just how to caddy. We learned how to be men and gained a sense of belonging by being in each other's presence. Most of my memories of being a caddy were enjoyable and adventurous. They were memories that I would treasure for the rest of my life.

There was only one time that I can recall that brought about a negative connotation in my mind of being a caddy. The family had begun to hit a very, very low point financially. It was getting harder and harder for Daddy to put food on the table and keep a roof over our heads. Mom came up with the idea that I could ask one of the rich white men that I caddied for a loan. I tried to talk Mom out of the idea, giving every reason that I could think of, but she persisted. I was so embarrassed. It felt like I had reached one of the lowest points in my life.

Obeying my mother's wishes, I asked one of the white men, who I caddied for, for a loan. At first, he gave the impression that he was more embarrassed than I was because he did not have a lot of money on hand. Then he offered me a few dollars retrieved from his pocket. I was so humiliated and embarrassed. I took the money and held my head down as I walked away. I never wanted to be in that position again, ever! I think that is why I had made up my mind to work hard and to be successful in whatever career path I took.

Our family was faced with many more hardships to come, yet, we never failed to hold on to hope. It was hope that always kept our heads held high and allowed us to keep our eyes on the light that could always be found on the other side.

# Chapter 4
# ASHES TO ASHES

---

## *The Flaming Inferno*

---

One night our family experienced something that significantly changed our life. It all began late one evening in our home. It was around our bedtime, and two of my sisters and I were awake, sitting by the fireplace, making conversation like any other evening that we had before. My other sisters and brothers were in bed, asleep in their bedroom on the other side of the house. My dad was in the living room, trying to tweak the kerosene heater, making some adjustments here and there. On this particular evening, my dad decided that he was going to pour more coal oil into the kerosene heater. Out of nowhere, we heard a loud boom sound! And almost immediately, things changed. We had no idea where the noise had come from or what had just happened. We later discovered it was the sound of the kerosene heater exploding.

At once, the house became engulfed in flames. I opened the door to the room that we were in, and I immediately saw flames everywhere. In no time at all, the explosion turned our home into a large flame that soon became a major inferno that ravaged the entire house. I ran out the front of the house and dashed around to the back of the house to wake the rest of the family. My mother and my other sisters were able to get out of the house through the front door. Meanwhile, Dad was trying to put the fire out. Initially, Freddie and I tried to help with putting the fire out but quickly realized that the flames were spreading too quickly, and there was no way that we were going to be able to extinguish the flames. Back then, there were no fire hydrants to draw water from. There were no firefighters or fire stations to call for help and no 911 calls to be made. There was nothing. Some of the neighbors were in a panic, and they were hurrying about and watering down their homes to the best of their ability to prevent their homes from being engulfed too.

My dad was still inside, trying to fight the flames. I called out to my dad to come out of the house. By this time, the smoke in the house had become so thick. More and more, the house continued to fill with layers of thick black smoke. There was a searing heat that followed, as the flames began overtaking each room in the house. My dad finally concluded, as we all had, that it was a lost cause and ran out of the house yelling, "Get out of the house everybody!" We could all hear the panic in his voice. By then, everyone was out of the house and standing at a distance from the house, watching the house go up in flames. The fire was so bright that it lit up the night sky like a Fourth of July celebration. Smoke could be seen cascading from blocks away. It traveled across the midnight skies and made its way through the neighborhood.

The fire soon overtook and swallowed up every inch of our home until it became completely consumed by fire. We stood there watching and listening hopelessly to the crackling of the kindle and the sound of the fire taking down each part of the house. Other neighbors gathered around to console us as we watched the remains of our home burn to the ground. The sound of burning wood crackling intensified throughout what seemed like the entire night. The structure lit up in sections like red coals on fire then took its time transforming itself into black dust. It burned down to the foundation right before our eyes. All that we could utter was "God help us!"

As children, you don't know what to think when your world is turned upside down like this. I remember thinking to myself "What are we going to do"? I could never have thought of something like this ever happening. The look on my mother's face was the look of despair but at the same time of hope. With a stern look, she held my sister close to her bosom and, after a few solemn swallows, she found the words to say "I'm just glad everybody is okay, and no one was harmed. We can thank God for that."

The next morning, our family walked through the remains of what was once our house only to find ashes and soot burying the partial remains of our home. The back half of the house was now a pile of ash and, as the wind blew, ashes fluttered in the air like confetti. The ash traveled across the grass and landed like snow. We looked upon the devastation, still in disbelief that this had happened to us. We all were faced with the reality that what was once our home was gone.

The American Red Cross helped out the family after the fire with clothes and other items that we were in desperate need of. We also received some help from a few people within our community. One of the community neighbors allowed us to rent out a small section of his house for a while. Keep in mind, this was a very small house already. Our family, being added to the equation, kept everyone cramped for space, but we made the best out of the situation. We were not used to living in such cramped conditions, but we managed to survive living this way for several months.

We didn't know where or what we were going to do moving forward, but as usual, our daddy had a plan. One day, out of nowhere, that plan rolled right into our now-vacant lot where our old house stood. My dad bought a rebuilt older house from an adjourning neighborhood area, which was a mining town, and had it hauled to our lot in Cape Town. The mining town homes were typically structured and came with a tin roof. This one also came with a porch with wood support posts on each side of the porch. This house only had three rooms, and the rooms were very small. It had a kitchen and a living room as well.

As fortunate as I knew that we were to have a roof over our heads at all, sometimes we did not feel so fortunate. The kids made fun of us for a long time, calling us the kids that lived in the "tin roof house." Eventually, we got over the kids teasing us about our new house, and life went on as normal. Like any other family that has gone through this sort of tragedy, we survived it. We made the necessary adjustments along the way. Nobody had much breathing room from one another, This gave me an excuse to be out of the house more. My mother never had to worry about me. She knew exactly where I would be; I was in the cow pasture, practicing my golf swing.

## *Cow Pastures*

Over time, I became an experienced caddy and was inspired to play golf as well. I didn't know of any public golf course where black people would be allowed to play and practice. Luckily, I was creative, and I found a place where I could go from time to time and practice my swing. This was perfect open greenery, subtle slopes, and hilly terrain. So I went to work and built my own golf course in the back area of our house, in an unused cow pasture. I was able to lay out the holes on my makeshift golf course, which was very similar to a par-three golf course. I smoothed out the red clay dirt areas with a shovel, and I laid out the golf holes. I substituted cans for the holes and made the flagpoles out of branches and plain white rags.

I bought some discarded second hand golf clubs at the pro shop at Mountain Brook Club. I was restricted to playing with iron clubs due to the short distances between the holes in the cow pasture. Picture this: the shortest hole was 120 yards and the longest approximately 170 yards.

The word got around town about my homemade golf course, and several caddy mates and schoolmates began walking the shortcut path from Stacy Hollow to Cape Town with their golf clubs in hand to play pickup golf competitions on my cow pasture golf course. It had become a big hit! We played for nickels and dimes. We spent many evenings out in that pasture, playing until the sun went down, taking small breaks here and there. On our breaks, we purchased BB brand soda pop and cookies from what was left of my father's grocery store.

I must have practiced for hours and hours in that cow pasture. I started out taking practice swings. Over time, I began developing a swing routine for the golf course and creating a tempo and muscle memory to hit quality shots.

I often hit between 50 and 400 balls in my practice sessions. I set a routine and mentally focused on doing the same swing routine for every shot. I developed a full backswing and an inside-out powerful downswing.

*S. Morris Holloway Jr., age 15*

I learned early in age that golfing was my thing. It was something that I was motivated to pursue and that I never wanted to stop doing. Whatever else I pursued in life, I knew golf was going to be a part of my life.

### The Power of Prayer

My mother was a woman who believed in the power of prayer. She shared this wisdom with all of her children.

If you can do nothing else, you can always pray!

James 5:16b

**16** The prayer of a righteous person is powerful and effective.

# Chapter 5
# GROWING PAINS

*The Diagnosis*

I faced many challenges on the road to manhood. One of those challenges came while I was still a student in junior high school. I was around thirteen or fourteen years of age when I developed a peculiar feeling in the left bicep area of my arm. It started out as just a cramp. I told my mother about it, but no one thought it was too serious at first. For the most part, it was only seen as an annoyance. After a few days, the cramp became more painful, and my arm began to swell. Over time, the swelling grew and along with the swelling came more pain.

With the increase in the pain and swelling in my arm, my mother took me to the University Hospital emergency room. The hospital diagnosed me with having an abscess in my left upper arm. No one knew why the abscess had developed. The doctor told Momma that I would have to have surgery to have the abscess drained and removed from my arm. I was very scared of what might happen. I remember praying a lot during this time and trying my best to keep a positive outlook.

The surgeon performed the surgery, making a seven-inch incision into the area where they drained the pus and cleaned out the infected tissue from my arm. After the surgery, I was kept in the hospital for a few weeks. At the time of my discharge from the hospital, my arm had not healed. In my opinion, I was discharged prematurely. I still had an "open wound" that had to be attended to. They simply dressed my arm and sent me home, telling my mother to do the same. My mother had no medical experience in caring for a wound of this nature. Now, this would never be heard of today.

Jim Crow laws affected many black people in this way. Black people were used to not receiving adequate medical treatment, even to the point of being forced to give up their bed if it were needed by a white person. The black facilities did not house as many beds for African Americans, which led to many African American people being turned away, sent home prematurely, or even denied proper health-care. So, there I was being sent home with an open wound. My mother did the best she could. She couldn't afford to buy sterile bandages, so she used some of our cotton rags that we had, and she sanitized them with boiling water. She folded them flat and heated them on top of the stove. Then, she wrapped those rags around my wound in substitution for sterilized gauzes, to keep the wound clean. She didn't know how difficult it was to keep the wound sterile. She also did not realize that without sterile gauzes the return of the infection was inevitable.

As you might imagine, my arm became infected again. It was a scary situation, especially for a young man of my age, to deal with. I still recall how my arm, when pressed against my body, would release yellow pus, and the pus would flow from the wound down my arm. It was very frightening and uncomfortable, not to mention embarrassing. I managed to keep it concealed as much as possible. A short time after the first surgery, I was informed that I would have to have another surgery. At this point, I became diagnosed with osteomyelitis. This simply meant that the infection had "gone to the bone." The doctor went ahead and performed the same surgery, only this time he had to take out some of the bone and infected tissue.

Though my mother was not the most medically inclined person, she could get a prayer through. So she prayed and prayed for my arm to heal. She encouraged me to believe in my healing as well. I believed, and I prayed. And when I was able to, I purchased my own sterile gauzes so that I could care for my arm properly. Over time, the oozing of pus decreased, and one day it just stopped altogether.

By the time I entered my last year of high school, my arm had fully healed, but the scar never went away. That's something I will have forever and take to the grave with me. Today, I realize how fortunate I was. I know now that back then they did not know as much as they know today medically, and black people were not always given adequate medical treatment when necessary. I was blessed to have been able to retain my arm and to still be able to hit golf balls as I had so much enjoyed doing. The challenge of overcoming this frightening incident is what made me decide to pursue a career in the medical field.

## *Little Bullies*

I think that each kid at some time in life will run into someone that he or she considers to be a bully. I can recall a couple of specific run-ins that I had with some bullies in my neighborhood. One of those bullies was a little closer to my own age. This young man's name was Jerome Parnell who was much bigger than me. I had a small build and stature and got picked on by many kids. I was usually one of the smallest guys in the group.

All of the neighborhood kids were outside playing in a park area in the community. He decided he was going to pick on me. He started wrestling me and throwing me around. I kept telling him to stop, and of course, he didn't. Once he let me go, I ran home, grabbed my Red Ryder BB gun, and headed back to the park to catch up with him. He was still out there with three of my other buddies. They told him he better run because I was coming back with my gun.

When I returned he just stood there looking at me. I'm sure he didn't expect what was going to happen next. I pulled out my BB gun and unleashed a barrage of bb's from the gun out on him. He eventually got a hold of the bb gun by wrestling it away from me and told me, "You better go home." To my surprise, he gave me the gun back, and I started shooting him again. The guys were all laughing. They thought it was hilarious that I shot him with my Red Ryder BB gun. After shooting off many rounds, I finally backed away from him and headed back home. I made sure to keep my eyes on him, as I slowly backed away and made my way back home.

Weeks later, Jerome and I became friends. He respected me for having the courage to stand up to him and fight back. He commended me for being brave enough to fight back and stand up to him. This was a friendship that lasted for some years and one of my bully stories that had a happy ending.

## Evil Eyes

There was another bully, who came across my path in life, who did not have such a happy ending. This was my encounter with the neighborhood bully by the name of Otis Stevens. Otis was a very dark-skinned young man whose eyes always looked bloodshot red. It made it appear to many that he was always tired or something. When I looked at him with those red eyes, I always thought of him as evil. One day, some of the neighborhood boys were all hanging out and about on the block a few blocks from the corner. This was something that we did on many occasions. Once again, I was one of the smaller kids in the group.

A lot of the boys in the neighborhood had been hanging out for some time that day when Otis decided that he was going to pick on me. Nobody liked Otis, including me. All of a sudden, he grabbed me and began tossing me about. I was no match for wrestling with him. Otis was way bigger than I was. He must have weighed almost twice as much as I did. But I did all that I could do at the time.

In between the wrestling and scuffling, we got verbal and passed some words to one another, and he yelled out threats to hurt me and my family. As soon as I heard that, I ran all the way home and ran unto the house and got up on the stool and pulled down my dad's shotgun that he kept hanging over the door. It was all that I could do to keep back the tears. Yet a few began to escape down my cheek and dribble onto my pants. With a few wipes around my nose and clearing my throat, I clicked the gun to make sure that there were bullets in it. As my feet hit the floor and I proceeded to the door with the shotgun in my hand, from out of nowhere I felt my mother's firm hand as she grabbed my arm, holding it down in position. She asked me what I was doing. I told her I was going to shoot Otis.

As I continued for the door, with one loud shout my mother yelled, "Stop! I said to stop!" It was then that I stopped in my tracks, held my head down, and slowly released the shotgun to my mother. I knew she was right. I could not and should not do what my heart was telling me to do. I was filled with so much pain. This was the only way that I thought that I could be rid of that pain at the time.

My mother tried to console me. The tears continued rolling down my cheek as I yanked my arm back from my mother in resistance. "Not this way," my mother shouted, "Not this way. He will get his one day. You can be sure of that, but you can't handle it this way," she said, knocking me upside the head for having even suggested the idea. My bottom lip shivered, and as my eyes once again filled with water. I had no choice but to release those tears as well.

Instead of going out that door, I went back into my room, sat down on my bed, and began to think. That's all I did for some time. I was glad that my mother was there for me that day. I thought about what could have been. Today, I think about how my life could have taken a much different path had she not been there. The bottom line was that, if not for the grace of God, there go I.

Otis never did change his ways. Years later, Otis bullied some other boy, but this time the story took another turn. That boy went home and got his father's shotgun. He later returned. No one was there to stop that young man as he chased Otis down and shot him in the back. Otis was left paralyzed and confined to a wheelchair for the rest of his life. A short time after that incident, Otis' house caught on fire. His body was later found burned to death inside of the house. We assumed that he was unable to escape the house after the house caught fire and was engulfed in the flames. This happened about three years after I left Birmingham.

Over the years I referred to him as the red-eyed devil. Many said he got what was coming to him. To this day I don't understand why he was so mean, but I do know his meanness cost him a lot—even possibly his life.

## Black Code and Jim Crow Laws

*After the civil war came to an end, in resistance against racial equality, southern states began passing laws called Black Codes. Black Codes were a series of discriminatory laws aimed at restricting the freedom of black people. These laws forced African Americans to continue to work on plantations as cheap labor after slavery was abolished.*

*These laws varied from state to state. Under these codes, African Americans could be required to sign yearly labor contracts; if they refused, they could be fined, arrested, or forced to work without pay. These codes limited what jobs African Americans could hold and the kind of property they could own, rent, or lease. These codes could deprive blacks the right to vote, the right to own or carry weapons, and the right to serve on juries.*

*In 1867, the Reconstruction Act came into effect that required all states to uphold the Fourteenth Amendment that extended citizenship to African Americans as well as the Fifteen Amendment that gave black men the right to vote.*

*Black codes were a big part of why blacks pushed for racial equality in the Constitution. However, instead of blacks getting equality, they ended up getting "separate but equal" treatment. Black Codes became the springboard for "Jim Crow laws," which legitimized segregation.*

# Chapter 6
# THE CAMPAIGN

*Segregation*

"Jim Crow" laws were passed by Birmingham lawmakers between 1944 and 1951. This covered all public arenas, such as restaurants, bus stations, and any private interactions. These laws were eventually overturned by the federal Civil Rights Act of 1964. Examples of segregation laws include:

**SECTION 369. SEPARATION OF RACES**

It shall be unlawful to conduct a restaurant or other place for the serving of food in the city, at which all white and colored people are served in the same room, unless such white and colored persons are effectually separated by a solid partition extending from the floor upward to a distance of seven feet or higher, and unless a separate entrance from the street is provided for each compartment.

**SECTION 597. NEGROES AND WHITE PERSONS NOT TO PLAY TOGETHER**

It shall be unlawful for a negro and a white person to play together or in company with each other in any game of cards or dice, dominoes or checkers.

**SECTION 1002. SEPARATION OF RACES.**

Every common carrier engaged in operating streetcars in the city for the carrying of passengers shall provide for each car used

**for white and colored passengers, separate entrances and exits to and from such cars in such a manner as to prevent intermingling of the white and colored passengers when entering or leaving such a car.**

**And it shall be unlawful for any person, contrary to the provisions of this section providing for equal and separate accommodations for the white and colored races on streetcars, to ride or attempt to ride in a car or a division of a car designated for the race to which such person does not belong.**

In 1954, segregation was legally enforced throughout Alabama. Segregation socially separated citizens based on race and went beyond separating black schools and white schools. It extended as far as the separation of black and white graveyards. It denied African Americans the right to vote and created other forms of legal separation of races, but most dangerously, it allowed Whites to get away with continued violations being inflicted upon African American people. It made them feel as if they could continue with the threats, economic oppression, and the use of intimidation tactics on African Americans without consequence.

This not only affected African Americans, but it also affected those in close association with them. People who had belonged to black churches or interacted primarily with African Americans socially were recognized as being black people by Alabama's legal system, even if they were not "black" people, and were treated as such.

Words like nigger, niggard, colored, and blacks were used quite frequently in the presence of an African American, on TV, and just about everywhere else. These were acceptable terms used when addressing African Americans during this time. Once African Americans got the right to vote, the terms transitioned from nigger to niggard. Then from niggard to colored and from colored to Black.

Though segregation was very unjust for the black race, there were some positive outcomes of segregation for our African American communities. A lot of the African American institutes supported individual African Americans when necessary. Segregation allowed us to see our

African American business owners who had become successful in life up close all the time. It gave black African Americans a chance to shine without the presence and negativity from white people who tried to hold them down. Lord knows, we did not need that. We were doing enough of that to ourselves.

Birmingham, Alabama, was the premier segregated city in the South and maintained segregation for quite some time. Martin Luther King Jr. once said that "If he could desegregate Birmingham, Alabama, he could do it anywhere."

---

## Downtown

---

Over the years, I earned enough money from caddying and soliciting other odd jobs to buy my own school clothes. I took the bus from home to downtown Birmingham to shop for clothes. At this time, I had to board the bus in the small community of Wylam. This was the end of the line for the city transit services. When Blacks boarded Birmingham transit buses, we automatically went straight to the back of the bus which was where the black section was located. If there was no place for colored people to sit in the back, sometimes the driver would move the white sign up for more seats in the back or we had to stand up.

The younger kids would joke around and move the sign around sometimes. We looked at this as some sort of humorous thing to do. If we had been caught doing this, the bus driver could have called the police, and we would have been arrested. There was a time when one of the drivers saw us and told us kids to stop. Of course, we thought this was amusing and giggled about it under our breath. We never understood the seriousness of what we were doing. For us, this was just everyday life, and we were just having fun.

Downtown was segregated as well. You knew this by the signs posted "For whites only." Downtown consisted of a lot of white-owned businesses. A lot of these business owners lived in the Mountain Brook country club community. We were allowed to shop in these stores like white people; however, we were not allowed to try on any of the clothing for size, nor were we allowed to return any piece of clothing after it left the store. There were no black sales clerks, but there were black janitors and elevator attendants. There were some restaurants with sit-down eating counters inside the stores. Blacks were not allowed to sit down at these counters to eat.

## *The 4th Avenue Strip*

The Fourth avenue strip was considered to be a black area. The Carver Theater was a black-owned theater that was located on Fourth Avenue. Momma wouldn't allow us to go to the movies, but on occasions, I would slip away and catch a movie or two. If the theater was integrated, the whites were designated to sit on the bottom floor and the blacks on the top floor on the balcony of the theater. Sometimes the kids or young folks would throw popcorn down below on the white viewers.

Fourth Avenue was where a lot of our black-owned businesses were located. There were black businesses up this strip. There were black barbershops and mama and pop businesses. There were pawnshops and other small black businesses. You could always find a restaurant selling chitlins or pork chop dinners along the strip. They called it the "funky Broadway of Birmingham." And it was just that "Funky." This was a mean section of town where a lot of young men were known for carrying switchblades and knives for protection.

I purchased my school uniforms at the National Shirts Shop located right off Third Avenue. This was where I was able to purchase my clothes on the layaway plan. I bought all my Banlon & Cotton shirts and pants there, including any accessories. Every year, I made sure that I had everything I needed for school. Especially my senior year.

## *Blacks' Education*

I only attended three schools during my entire life in Birmingham, Alabama. I attended Gary Ensley elementary school, Edgewater

Middle school, and Jefferson County, Westfield High School, all in Birmingham, Alabama. All three of these schools were black-only schools. That meant all of the students were Blacks, and all of the faculty and staff were Blacks. Nothing but black faces could be seen, ranging from the darkest to the lightest skin tone. I often wondered what it would have been like to be in a classroom where all the students did not look alike, where all the students didn't have the same skin, hair, and ethnic culture. I wondered what the white schools looked like on the inside. What did the students look like? What did their teachers look like? What did the students learn? And what would it be like attending a white school every day?

It was a known fact that black schools received less funding and support than white schools. Black schools had secondhand books, and their materials and buildings were in far worse condition than the white schools. The black teachers were paid less and had larger classes than the white schools as well. Our black teachers' duties went far beyond academic instruction; they were often required to use their own funds to help their students both inside and outside the classroom. They placed the economic and social progress of their children in their hands.

Despite the difficulties many of our black teachers faced, they continued to be role models for their black students. They were successful black adults that had achieved a social status that we black people at that time considered to be acceptable and successful. Most of our black teachers owned homes and had nice cars. They exemplified pride in the black race and pride for their students.

Despite being categorized as one of the less-funded schools, we all felt like we got a very good education. We had a lot of fun while learning as well. One year, we studied "Macbeth" in our English literature class. I as well as many of the other students thought that it was exciting as we listened to recordings. We were every bit happy to see the television version of the play and view films of Shakespeare's greatest tragedy. And we were even more enthused when we had the pleasure of reading the play. I think many of the students found the writing to be even better than the TV version. I thought it was one of the most rewarding experiences that had occurred during class dramatizations.

After these dramatizations, each student was challenged with writing an analysis of a character in the play.

There were a lot of club membership opportunities for students. I was a member of the journalist club. We also had several committees, and I was a member of the civil defense committee. All of the class instructors and officers of course were black. We called them the 12-D. Fannie Terry was the financial secretary; Wayne Jeffreys, business manager; Gwendolyn Mack, treasurer; Joyce Lawrence, chaplain; Nathan Green, sergeant of arms; Barbara Ryan, vice president; Mary Wilson, secretary; Shelby Brown, second business manager; Annie Danner, president; and Mrs. Anita Quinn, instructor.

## The Senior Class of Westfield High School, 1962

My entire senior class body consisted of 196 students. Most of us had known each other and attended the same schools for most, if not all, of our childhood. Senior year brought about many exciting challenges. One of those challenges materialized when one of the students from my community nominated me for class president. Becoming the class president was never at the forefront of my thoughts; nonetheless, I accepted the nomination as well as the challenge. This was the beginning of my campaign for running for class president.

During my senior year in high school, I was very popular. The Holloway name was very well known. People never forgot my dad's grocery store, and everyone knew who the Holloway kids were. There were eight of us children, and we all attended the same school. So, the name Holloway stayed on the roster at these schools for a long time.

A lot of people knew me, and a lot of the students thought that I was very smart. I wasn't all that smart; I just did what we were supposed to do—I studied. As a result of my studying, when it came time to take the test, I passed the test with flying colors.

I knew that in running for president I was going to have to sell my qualifications to the senior class. The boy I was running against was very well known as well. His name was Shelby Brown. Shelby was only popular with the girls. He was a real light-complexioned guy and had a head full of black curly hair that made him stand out. He got a lot of attention because of his looks, especially from some of the girls. I remember overhearing one of my peers saying, "Oh, Square doesn't stand a chance going up against Shelby Brown for class president. He might as well forget it." Hearing that got my juices going, and I was disappointed to hear him say that. After all, I wasn't a stranger to good looks myself. I stood five foot nine and weighed about 140 pounds. I was slim, tall, dark, and handsome. I was also considered a very likable guy by many of my peers, not to mention my name was already popular. I was ready to give Shelby a run for the position.

I started planning my campaign right away. What that guy didn't know was that I had a secret weapon, and I planned on using it to my advantage. I created a lot of posters that were pretty simple and passed out a few handouts to the students. These were some of the fairly easy tasks to complete for the campaign. Then each nominee had to prepare a speech that they would give in front of the class body. I figured this would be the real challenge.

I decided that I was not going to make the yearly campaign promises that most other students made when running for office. Instead, I focused on my qualifications and previous experiences. At the end of my speech, I decided to add a catchy phrase or slogan that I hoped would catch the ears of the student body and help them to understand my goal for our senior class. Since my name was popular and very peculiar, I decided to use my name in the slogan. I came up with a slogan that would gain recognition and be memorable. This was one time that the name Square would work to my benefit.

On the day of our speech, the student body gathered in the auditorium where Shelby Brown and I both prepared to make our campaign speeches. Shelby gave his speech first, and then I followed. My speech was concise and to the point. The speech went a little something like this:

"Welcome student body. My name is Square Morris Holloway, and I'm running for Senior Class President. From the earliest times, leaders of men have had outstanding qualities that called them out to lead others. Qualities such as honesty, perseverance, and a positive outlook... I do not claim to have all of these qualities, but I do possess some of them.

"My ninth grade class felt that I was honest and elected me the treasure of their class. My tenth grade class thought that I was smart and voted for..." I went on to list all of my achievements throughout school so that the student body would know about my past experience.

The highlight of the day came at the very end of my speech as I summed up my speech with "Remember, *"Vote for Square, let's get somewhere!"* This catchy phrase grew within the student body and I think allowed me to get the best in the campaign. *"Vote for Square, let's get somewhere!"*, *"Vote for Square let's get somewhere!,"* *"Vote for Square, let's get somewhere!"* After finishing my speech, the crowd gave out a loud applause and cheer. That catchy phrase continued to echo across the students' bodies, minds, and hearts. *"Vote for Square, let's get somewhere!,"* *"Vote for Square let's get somewhere!"* The girl I was dating at that time just knew I had won after she heard my speech.

The election of the Student Council officers was held on Tuesday, October 31. The following students were elected officers of the Student Council: Square Holloway, president; George Forrest, vice president; Josephine Horton, secretary; Francine Moore, assistant secretary; Robert Bivins, treasurer; and Williams Smedley, sergeant-at-arms. I won the election by a landslide. It was all I could do to keep my composure when I passed by that peer that made the comment about me not standing a chance, as well as my opponent in the halls that year. Like I said, I was always up for a challenge.

Being class president came with a lot of perks. I could get out of having to go to a lot of my classes if I wanted to. I never did. I enjoyed being at school, especially as class president. I was proud of the achievements of the student council that year I was class president. After nine months of very hard work, the student council was able to look back at what we had accomplished, such as the litter campaign that we launched. We sponsored activities and made enough money to send two representatives to the Alabama State Meeting of Student Councils that took place in Mobile. We also organized such events as the Valentine Ball and the Booker Brown Day.

There was one project in particular that highlighted my tenure as student council president. The council was allowed to raise funds by sponsoring movies on Fridays and after-school dances for the student body. We acquired enough money to launch a beautification program for the campus grounds. By the end of the spring, the blossoming flowers gave each council member much to be proud of. This turned out to be my very best year in High school. I was also selected to appear in the *(1961–62) Edition of Who's Who Among Student Leaders In High Schools of America* From Westfield High School the same year.

There's an old saying that time flies when you're having fun. Before I knew it, the entire senior class and I were contemplating graduation. My time at Westfield High had been fulfilling, but I was anxious to leave the cultural restraints of Birmingham, Alabama. As the months began rolling along, I knew I had to start planning for the next steps in my life. I was not sure right away what I was going to do after graduation. As fate would have it, a few months before graduation, I received a letter from my sister about this great opportunity she had stumbled across during her internship. My sister Marcia was in her third year at Knoxville College which required an internship in medical technology at Mercy Hospital in Springfield, Ohio. She discovered that Mercy Hospital was accepting applications from high school graduates for a one-year program in medical technology. She suggested that I apply.

I knew very little about medical technology, but I went ahead and wrote a letter to the lab director at the hospital inquiring about the possibility of my entry into their medical technology program. I sent the letter to Mercy Hospital, to the attention of Dr Mary P. Hunter, the director of the laboratory.

---

Letter to Mercy Hospital Laboratory
March 22, 1962
To Dr. Mary Hunter,

Mercy Hospital Laboratory
1343 North Fountain Ave,
Springfield, Ohio

Dear Dr. Hunter,

I am a prospective graduate of the class of 1962 at Westfield High School in Birmingham Alabama. I am interested in your school of technology. I would like to apply for entrance in the school at the earliest possible date after my graduation. Please send me an application and other necessary material for applying. In addition, please send me an outline of your school's program.

I would appreciate hearing from you as soon as possible.

Respectfully yours,

Square Morris Holloway,
Training Department
PS: I would like for you to know one of your present students Marcia Holloway is my sister.

---

I received a letter from Ms. Edith Cassidy, the chief technologist at Mercy Hospital laboratory a week later, which included an information package and an entry form. Not long after returning my application to the hospital, I was notified that I had been accepted into the program. I could hardly contain myself in my excitement over the prospect of leaving Alabama. This was the beginning of a new beginning for me. It was also a very big part of what was soon to be my future.

As quickly as that year came, it went, and on Wednesday evening, May 13, 1962, I became a proud graduate from Jefferson County Westfield High School in Birmingham Alabama. Three days after my graduation I boarded a Greyhound bus and headed north to Springfield, Ohio, where my sister Marcia was eagerly awaiting my arrival.

In my wallet was a folded piece of paper with the name and address of one of my history teachers' mothers. I promised her that I would look her up if time permitted. Only time would tell. All that I knew for sure at that moment was that I was ready for the next chapter in my life, and *I was on my way!*

Senior Year 1962

*Square Morris Holloway Jr.*

*I left Birmingham with a suitcase,*
*and a farewell kiss from the family.*

## Part 2

# THE MAN
# AND THE DREAM

*Black Migration*

O ver a four decade period millions of African Americans residing in the rural Southern United States migrated to the urban Northeast, Midwest, and West parts of the United States. Many African Americans felt it necessary to make this move due to the racial segregation and discrimination taking place in those regions as well as seeking better opportunities for education and career advancements elsewhere.

## A Whole New World

I had never seen black and white men and women attending the same school, not to mention the same class. This was a culture shock for me. We sat next to one another, we talked to one another, and we learned with one another while in the same classes together. I had always wondered how I would adapt to this newfound experience.

# Chapter 7
# A WHOLE NEW WORLD

---

*Becoming a New Man*

---

A s I crossed the border into Ohio, riding the Greyhound bus, I glanced outside the windows and got lost in the cornfields. I was surprised to see so many tall cornfields disappearing in the blur of the horizon. We must have passed acres and acres of cornfields. What may have been just an everyday sight for many was more than a wonder for me. While passing the sight of those tall and slinky stalks of corn, I thought of the new life that was set before me. I watched as those tall stalks lean against the summer breeze as we passed them by. I felt their excitement as they appeared to be dancing with one another in the wind. In my imagination, it was as if they were celebrating the journey with me.

As we passed through the inner city, I became astonished by the substantial amount of bars that we passed along the way. I saw one, two three, and four. I thought, *"Wow this sure must be a very liberal state."* I had never seen so many bars in one place at one time. Soon the bus pulled up to the station. I continued peering out the window until we were given the word to depart from the bus. I didn't see anything that looked like it did in Birmingham, Alabama. I had entered a whole new world.

I felt like Dorothy in Oz as I took my first step off that bus and planted them onto the pavement. And there I was stepping on the yellow brick road and making my way to the magical wizard who could make all my dreams come true. It felt like a fairy tale. Being in Springfield gave me a sense of freedom that I had never felt before.

There was also a sense of fear and joy. I knew I was officially an adult now and would soon experience all those things that come along with independence, adulthood, and freedom.

The moment I arrived at Mercy Hospital, I knew my life was about to change. I sat outside the lobby area in the hospital, waiting for my sister and looked around in high anticipation. I observed the blood donor activities taking place next door. I watched as one of the donor's blood flowed from his arms and down into the glass vacuum quart-size bottle. The blood flowed through the tubing and bubbled as it slowly filled the bottle. I felt a wave of nausea hit me. I immediately sulked back in my seat as I continued watching as the bottle filled into capacity. I watched the technician as she disconnected the tubing from the donor's arm and provided the donor with a glass of fruit juice. The donor was then advised to sit for about thirty minutes before leaving the building. I was petrified and overly excited all at the same time. I knew this was the place for me. My eyes were stuck on this technician, like glue, following her as she removed the blood from the room, transporting it to the main blood bank for processing.

Shortly after, my sister Marcia finished her assigned duties, came out of the lab, and introduced me to her coworkers and the chief tech, Edith Cassidy. Before I arrived in Springfield, my sister and I had decided that she would introduce me as Morris instead of Square. This would eliminate a lot of inquiries as to where the name Square came from. The curiosity of many in regard to this matter was something I had to deal with most of my life, and I felt like it was time for a change.

Edith Cassidy and Dr. Hunter informed me of how my classes would be set up and that I would be working alongside some of the more seasoned technicians. I was also informed I would be attending classes daily and given daily activities to complete. This gave me some insight as to what I could expect. I knew right away that there were going to be some challenges, but I felt like I was up for the challenge.

Mercy Hospital was a Catholic hospital at this time. Sister Amobolis was one of several nuns who worked at the hospital and headed different departments. Sister Amobolis managed all the lab activities alongside Dr. Hunter and her staff. All the nuns wore black-and-white habits. There was one priest who accompanied the nuns. The priest was responsible for managing the spiritual activities. They had their own headquarters on campus.

The students in the lab came from all over the country. There were some from local colleges, and then you had foreign students who came from places like the Philippines and Nigeria. After graduation, some of the foreign students stayed and worked as staff technicians or became a part of Mercy Hospital's staff. Others went back to their native country and continued their education there. A lot of these students were very smart, coming from the higher echelons of their societies. Each group generally had their campus. The Filipino students had their own living quarters. The female students had to have chaperones whenever they went off campus or away from the hospital. Each student was required to wear a uniform to school while attending lab classes. Our uniform consists of Ben Casey–style white shirts, white pants, white lab coats, and a tie with white shoes. I remember feeling like this was like a dream come true for me.

The first day of class opened my eyes to things I had never seen before. Throughout my education, I had only attended schools where there were only black students. This was the first time I would be attending class with both white and black students. This was a culture shock for me. I had never seen black and white men and women attending the same school, not to mention the same class. We sat next to one another and talked to one another while in the same classes together. All that I had ever wondered about how this would be all those years was now coming to fruition. I was allowed to be taught in the same capacity and to compete with a white person in a learning environment. This was an opportunity I had not been given before.

This was a wonderful experience for me, yet it caused me to have to study even harder. I had to be sure that I stayed competitive with the other students. I always felt as if I had to be better to achieve what I set out to achieve. Regardless of the challenges, I felt so fortunate to be able to attend this school and to have been given this opportunity. I was a very high achiever and I made A's and B's consistently, throughout my training. Things only got better once I became established. I was excelling in all of my classes. I made the best grades in our class by doing what I had done most of my life. I studied the assigned material and obtained good grades as a result. I found myself enjoying school more and more.

## *Living Quarters*

While attending tech school, I stayed with a lady by the name of Lillian Moody. Ms. Moody was an elderly widow who had roots in the South and lived in Ohio. She and her husband left South Carolina and moved to Ohio with their son. Her sister had settled in Birmingham, my hometown, and she said her sister, Ms. Moody, would be happy to provide room and board for me while I attended school in Ohio. Ms. Moody was a very thin elderly lady about five foot, nine inches tall. She had a head full of gray hair that was neatly propped and pinned up on the top of her head. She looked like she was somewhere in her eighties. As she walked, there was a sense of pride in her step.

Ms. Moody was known for being a very pious Christian lady who took pride in her church and her church activities. She was well known around Springfield due to being a homeowner for several years. Not many black people owned their own homes then. I remember the first time she set eyes on me. She looked me over from head to toe before showing me to my living quarters, which was a small bedroom that had a small dresser and a small window. She allowed me access to the kitchen. I had the privilege of morning coffee as well. My daily meals were normally Chef Boyardee spaghetti and meatballs, and ravioli for dinner.

To look upon her house you would think of a small box. It wasn't much to look upon. I mean it wasn't anything fancy, but it was home. It was located on Center Street, about three blocks from downtown and about five miles away from the hospital. Center Street was one of the main roads leading to the hospital. I woke up early every day and walked to the hospital. It was a long walk, but I got used to it. And it was something that I had to do to attend class. It wasn't long before moving into Ms. Moody's that I discovered that Edith Cassidy, the chief tech, lived a few blocks from her house. One morning, as Ms. Cassidy was passing by Ms. Moody's house on her way to the hospital she saw me walking and she stopped and offered me a ride. She said to me, "There's no sense in you walking when I ride right by Ms. Moody's house."

Cassidy was an old maid that had never married. She was a slim woman about five foot, nine inches, with blond hair and a pointed nose. She lived in a black neighborhood. Though many Whites had moved away to get away from the Blacks who had branched out into that area, she didn't see any need for moving. The houses in her vicinity were very well maintained, and she was content and satisfied.

She became quite a blessing in my life. She and I would form a lifelong relationship of mutual respect. As the chief tech, she had a big influence on my career path. She noticed how much I applied myself in class and my potential for becoming a tech right away. She grew very fond of me and took me under her wing, so to speak. She started driving me to and from the hospital every day. I no longer had to do that five-mile walk. I didn't mind the walk when this was my only option, but it was a blessing when I didn't have to make that walk. If I overslept, she would honk her horn and wait for me on many occasions.

Edith Cassidy had become somewhat of a guardian angel. I remember that first Christmas I was away from home, she drove around Springfield and showed me all the Christmas lights in the different neighborhoods. It was truly fascinating. I hadn't seen anything like it. I thanked God in my prayers for sending her into my life.

There were times when I cut Ms. Cassidy's grass to make extra money. And when that was not enough to make ends meet, Cassidy would assign me to do blood donor collections. She drove some of us techs to different civic groups where we provided this service. We serviced groups like the JCs UFW, churches, and other civic-minded groups. This would allow me to earn as much as two dollars an hour. Performing blood draws on these blood donors gave me a world of experience. I became an excellent phlebotomist, and the word of my ability to perform difficult blood collection spread. Staff members then called on me to perform blood collections. I gained the reputation of being as good as some of the staff who were already established phlebotomists.

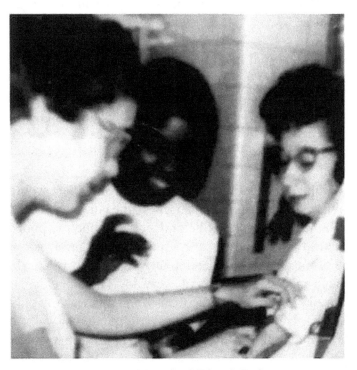

**Mercy Hospital Blood Lab**
**Mercy Hospital Medical Technologist Program**

My skills mandated me to be able to touch and feel for veins not always seen with the naked eye. I was known by my peers for being able to draw "blood from a turnip." On many occasions, some of the "in-house patients" requested me to draw their blood during the daily morning rounds.

They could care less about skin color. They made comments like, Give me that "tall, thin black guy" to draw my blood." Afterward, they marveled at how painless it was when I drew their blood.

## *Racism and Discrimination*

I thought this was a fairytale come true. However, it wasn't too soon before my fairy tale gave me a reality check. What I did not know at the time was that while discrimination was most prevalent and most evident in the South, it also existed in northern states. It was just not as obvious and in your face as it was in the South. I had a teacher who reminded me that prejudice did still exist even in a small town like Springfield, Ohio. Her name was Kathy Kalinos. Kathy was the micro-biology departmental supervisor for the lab classes I was attending. She was of Greek descent, a thin lady with black hair.

Her attitude toward the students was very harsh. I believe at the time that this was done to make the students tough. The term "crack the whip" was often expressed in her vocabulary. I felt as if she was particularly hard on me. I believed that she did not like black people.

One day, while getting ready for class, I found that my white pair of pants was still wet from being laundered so I substituted my khaki pants for the white pants. When Kathy Kalinos saw that I had khaki pants on and not white pants, she immediately told me I had to go back home and change into my white pants and that I could not return to the lab until I had white pants on. This was very disturbing to me seeing that there were white techs who did not have on white pants and were not made to go home and change. It was obvious that she was showing favoritism toward the Whites. She was a racist! And this was racism at its peak.

I was determined not to let her force me out of the program, so even though it was a several-mile walk, I walked back home and dried my white pants, and returned with my white pants on. When she saw that I had returned to class dressed in white pants, she gave a sort of smirk and said something like, "That's more like it." It was obvious she was trying to discourage me and keep me from finishing the program.

Had this been the only time that she was prejudiced against me, I might have been able to let it go but there was another occasion where Kathy made efforts to have me dismissed. She almost did. One day, a kitchen aide and I were having a conversation in the kitchen area, and Kathy happened to pass by. She felt like I should be in my assigned department and not talking to this young man. She verbally attacked me for having this conversation with the kitchen staff. She told me that I did not belong in that area and swore at me and then told me to get the h** back to my assigned department.

I was very embarrassed at what she did and what she said. I felt as if she was very abusive in her language and very belittling. The way that she approached me was unacceptable. At this point, I had had enough of her harassment and told her to her face that she did not have the right to speak with me in that manner. She told Sister Amobolis that I had disrespected her, and Sister Amobolis told me that I had to leave and upon my return I would have to talk to Dr. Hunter. Once I returned, Dr. Hunter s told me to go back to my department, and that was pretty much the end of that incident. I was sure that it was because Ms. Cassidy spoke up on my behalf and defended me.

What Ms. Kalinos did not realize at that time, but later discovered, was Cass was very fond of me, and we had befriended each other. When Kolinos realized that the chief tech, her boss, had taken me under her wings, she backed off and changed her attitude toward me. She even tried to befriend me as my schooling came to an end and I was pronounced a full-fledged technician. She asked me questions about civil rights demonstrations taking place in Birmingham to strike a conversation with me. Though I never dismissed her conversation, I was never interested in having in-depth conversation with her after how she treated me.

## The Techs

School continued to be interesting and, with each passing day, we learned something new. We worked side by side with the techs and went out in twos to the floors to draw blood from the in-house patients. All the techs went floor to floor drawing blood from patients. Of course, this was something I was acquainted with since I had been assisting with blood donations.

During this time, the night tech was resigning, and Cassidy and Hunter were looking to fill this position. Cassidy and Dr. Hunter decided to make me the night tech. Some of the other black staff techs were jealous when I was appointed to be the night tech. They made negative statements, such as "People better not get sick at night." It was hurtful to hear some of my black coworkers say something like that. This did not deter me. It made me more determined to become an accomplished tech.

Some of those techs who made negative statements sat for the American Medical Technologist registry and failed, whereas I passed on the first try! This southern man had proved himself again and beat the odds. These same techs later had to respect me for my talents. They did not realize I had a secret weapon. I had a praying mother. She also taught me how to pray!

---

## *Mr. and Mrs. Carter*

---

Though there were many other challenges I had to face while attending tech school, things always seemed to work out with God's help. I continued to work very hard to make ends meet while in school. I got a job as an orderly at the hospital, working evenings in the psychiatry ward. My assignment was to prepare beds as they became available for new patients. One day, while making the beds in the psychiatry ward, a nurse by the name of Ms. Hazel was observing me making one of the beds. She noticed that I was not making the beds the way they should have been made. She came in and started showing me the proper way.

She carefully removed the old sheets and placed them in the dirty bin. Then, she parachuted the bottom sheet and placed it on the bed, making sure that the centerfold of the sheet was right in the middle of the bed; then she secured the sides. She repeated the same technique using the second sheet, only this time she made sure that all the sides and ends were tucked under the mattress carefully. While she was making the bed, I looked at her because she looked like one of the old history teachers that I had at Westfield High School.

I told her, "You look so familiar." I couldn't think of who it was she looked like. So I told her, "You look a lot like one of my old history teachers at Westfield High School."

She laughed a bit as she continued making the beds and then she paused, looked at me, and asked me "What was your teacher's name?"

"Eliza Penny," I told her. Her eyes got as big as oranges, and she stumbled back almost falling over onto the bed.

"That's my cousin," she said, holding her hand close to her heart.

I pulled out a folded piece of paper from my wallet that Mrs. Penny, my history teacher had given to me. When I unfolded the paper, I read the person's name written on the paper. The name on the paper was Ms. Roseman. This was the name of a person that Mrs. Penny knew in Springfield and told me once I arrived in Springfield to get in contact with. When Mrs. Hazel heard this, she slumped down on the bed with her head down in disbelief. She said, "Morris, that is my mother." We were both amazed.

I hadn't forgotten about the paper in my wallet, but with not having any transportation to get around Springfield and with my heavy school schedule, I never really had the chance to pursue trying to find this person. Now, there I was speaking with her daughter. It was as if God sent her daughter to me because he knew I was unable to get to her.

We had a long conversation, and I listened as she began to reminisce about her career and how she got where she was. She talked about how she had been discriminated against and found it difficult to become a nurse and the barriers she had to become a black registered nurse. Black were not even allowed to walk on the same overpass as whites at that time at the hospital. This lady had been through a lot to get to where she was. I knew that, for me to succeed, I too was going to have to face some obstacles and challenges when it came to prejudice and that just because I left the South behind didn't mean that I had escaped the prejudice that resided within the minds of people.

Mrs. Carter later introduced me to her family. I met her husband Mr. Bill Carter and their six kids. They had four boys and two girls. Bill Jr., their oldest son was around my age. They invited me over to their house for dinner on many occasions, knowing that it was very seldom that I got a home cooked meal. I was always appreciative of them. It was Mr. Bill Carter who introduced me to black golfing in Springfield, Ohio. We teamed up and competed against Dayton golfers on several occasions. He and Demus Corley were instrumental in breaking down the color barriers that had kept Springfield golfers from playing on local public golf courses. It was a known fact that the local facilities in Springfield, Ohio, were just as segregated as any of the public facilities in the South.

Mr. Carter was a highly competitive man. He played all types of sports. He competed in bowling, tennis, and bridge tournaments as well as golfing. You name the sport, he knew how to play it and play it well. I learned a lot from him. He used to tell me the key to anything is to *never give up*! That stayed in my mind as I later began competing in golf. He instilled in me the importance of doing my best when competing, and he made me want to be my best by just being around him.

## *The Night Technician*

I completed tech school in 1963 and started working the night shift as a night tech almost immediately. Dr. Hunter ran the lab with a tight fist. "She was the boss!" Even the doctors in the hospital had to make appointments to confer with her. She was that important. Many times, I witnessed doctors bowing to her authority. So, anyone working this shift had to be on their p's and q's, so to speak.

She relied on her chief tech, Edith Cassidy, to serve in an advisory role, making sure that things stayed in top condition in her department. I worked the night shift primarily alone. I had to grow up practically overnight to fulfill these responsibilities, and there were a lot of responsibilities. This was considered to be a high-pressure job, and the lab staff knew this. I had the responsibility of providing service to the 375 in-house beds, plus covering the emergency room stat orders. I had to draw all the blood and run all the tests.

The daily routine for a tech looked something like this: routine, timed, and stat test orders described the priority of the ordered test. The first shift staff techs did the routine testing. These tests could be performed without much urgency as the blood was collected on the morning rounds. Timed test requests could be processed on a 24/7 basis. The in-house patients needed these tests performed to monitor the progress of their treatment. GI bleeders, patients on blood-thinning medication, such as heparin, would require their blood to be drawn and test results called to their doctor or the attending RN.

"Stat" test orders were of the highest priority meaning a life-threatening situation existed. Physicians were encouraged to select test orders from the designated "Stat" list. These basic tests helped the doctor make a reasonable diagnosis from the ailments displayed by ER patients and newly admitted in-house patients. The most often ordered tests were the CBC (complete blood count), urinalysis, glucose (blood sugar), cardiac profiles (hypertension tests), BUN and creatinine (kidney function tests), electrolytes (Na, K, Cl, $CO_2$), liver enzymes, pancreatic enzymes and any other metabolic test on the "Stat" list. Night techs would provide their test results on a Stat basis, meaning a quick turnaround time was expected. Of course, the night techs were also responsible for performing EKGs on a stat basis.

Along with these endeavors, I had some other things I had to focus on as well. Coming from the South, I had a southern tone and accent that was very evident when I spoke. I had to learn how to articulate my speech when answering the phones. The techs had to be professional in every aspect. So, I had to be very conscious of my demeanor. I was the face, hands, and voice of the lab department.

Since it was an overnight position, the bed located in the blood bank department was available for the night tech to sleep when his or her services were not needed. However, slow nights were becoming the exception rather than the rule. When I was able to take some time to lie down, I would place the phone bedside next to my ear in anticipation of incoming calls. When things got too overwhelming for me, I was instructed to call Cass, the chief tech, and she would come in and help out with the overload. Even she knew that the workload was reaching the point that a second night tech would eventually have to be hired.

Examples of some of those times were in trauma situations like gunshots wounds, stabbings, automobile accidents, and aneurysms. I would need that extra help in providing blood bank services. The duties of the night technician were continually growing, and the need to have someone to assist increased over time. More and more, the physicians depended on the laboratory to provide the test results to assist in providing their diagnosis.

## *Mercy, Mercy, Mercy*

Along with our many duties at the hospital, there were also just as many hospital dramas that occurred. One of the occasions involved one of the techs by the name of David. David was a model student who always carried himself in a very professional manner. Cass and all of his peers looked upon him as being the ideal staff tech. One day while on duty, David went to one of the floors to draw blood from a patient. This patient was an attractive young woman. I am not sure what the patient came to the hospital for, but David was supposed to be drawing blood from the patient and he told the patient that she had to completely *disrobe* in the process of collecting this patient's blood. After she disrobed, he fondled her breast.

Regardless of what he could have said about the accusation, we all knew there was no reason whatsoever why this patient had to be disrobed for him to draw her blood. This was more than inappropriate. This crossed every line a tech could cross and was one of the most unethical moves that he could have ever made. Right after the incident, one of the nurses found out what he had done to the patient and reported him to Cass. When word reached Cass, she was hot as all hot could get. She had entrusted this man with this position, and he went and did something like that. She called him a rotten SOB, and she called security and had him removed from the premises. She fired his behind right on the spot. He tried to explain, but he could forget it; no explanations were accepted. And he was never heard of again.

I worked in this position for over a year, and things were going very well. There were many challenges but nothing that I was not able to get past. One day I found out The Supremes, a Motown performing group, were coming to town, and they were having a concert at the Memorial center in Springfield. I purchased a ticket to go right away. So, I had my ticket well in advance before the concert. This was a once-in-a-life-time chance for me, I thought. It wasn't every day that the Supremes came to Springfield, Ohio, to perform. The Supremes were Motown's greatest up-and-coming performers at this time. It so happened that a day before the concert, I contracted a bug. My throat was sore, and I had a very high temperature. I was scheduled to work that night and due to not feeling well, I called in and informed them that I was sick and could not work that shift.

Of course, I took some medication and went to bed. By that evening, after resting up and letting the medication take effect, I began feeling somewhat better, so I decided I would go to the concert. After all, I had already paid for the tickets. I went to the concert, and the concert was great. I enjoyed being able to watch them perform live. And I was glad that I went. While I was at the concert, I ran into one of my white coworkers. This coworker ran straight to Cass and told her that they saw me at the concert, and the stuff hit the fan. The next day I got a call from Cass, telling me that I had to come in and see Dr. Hunter, the director. I knew right then it had to do with me not showing up for work but going to a concert.

This was my first run-in with Dr. Hunter. Dr. Hunter was a heavy-set lady, sort of stout with gray-white short hair, and spoke in a stern voice. She also had a manly disposition. When you saw her, she would usually be dressed in her whites. After hours, she dressed in a plaid shirt and blue jean overalls. She wore clothes like these while carrying out her favorite farm activities. She was known for being very firm but fair. She was also very dictatorial and had a no-nonsense personality. It was reported that she made the statement: "I could train a monkey to be a lab tech." She browbeat doctors on the medical staff and was quick to let them know that she ran the lab.

During my conversation with Dr. Hunter, I tried to explain to her that I had bought the ticket to the concert well in advance, But she told me that I had to "learn discipline," and if I were sick I should have stayed at home and not gone to the concert. She would accept no excuse for my not attending work. She gave me a one-day suspension. This was the first and last time that anything like this happened. The subject of this incident never came up between Cass and I ever again. She remained one of my most trusted confidants.

## A Change Is Coming

As close friends as Cass and I were, we didn't always agree with each other on matters of race. One of those matters involved the Civil Rights Movement. Opinions involving this topic caused some heated discussions between the two of us. Dr. Martin Luther King had become a known name all around the United States. I, like so many other black people at that time, felt like it was time for a change to take place in the United States. Equal rights for all Americans were well overdue black, white, or whatever ethnicity. It was time for America to live up to its creed.

Cass commented to the effect that Martin Luther King was trying to do too much too fast. She never came over to my side in agreement that it was time for a change regarding how blacks were treated and that Dr. Martin Luther King was doing what was necessary at the time to make those changes take place, but she did respect the fact that I expressed how I felt on the matter.

In 1963, Birmingham, Alabama, began one of the biggest campaigns of the Civil Rights Movement. This campaign was filled with many boycotts on companies that were segregated as well as lunch counter sit-ins and city hall marches. Blacks always tried to demonstrate in a peaceful protest that generally ended in violent attacks. Blacks protesting were subject to police brutality perpetrated with fire hoses and police dogs. This type of treatment was enforced on all the protestors, including women and children.

Despite the brutality and inhumanity of these events, they managed to move the hearts of many people as these attacks were viewed live on TV. The cry for justice and equality for all mankind surged throughout the country with each devastating occurrence. Some said that these events became the turning point for the nation. The nation had to live up to its creed. Some of the kids I went to school with, who were still living in Birmingham, were a part of that movement. I longed to be able to be a part of it as well.

In May of 1963, the local officials removed the "White Only" and "Black Only" signs from restrooms and drinking fountains in downtown Birmingham. This led to desegregated lunch counters, theaters, and markets. Demonstrators who had been jailed for their part in the protest had to be released. As big a victory as this was for Birmingham, it was only a small portion of what was to come. Some still had to deal with violent attacks from angry segregationists until things slowly came to a civil normalcy. It was a long time coming, but the change had to come, and thanks be unto God, it did!

After Martin Luther King Jr.'s assassination, Cass made the comment "I told you it would lead to no good." I remember being so angry at her for making that comment even to the point that my hands began to shake. I told her in a calm, stern voice, "Even though he was killed, he was right. His stand and his death did not take away the validity of his campaign. He did not die, nor would his death be, in vain."

At this time we heard all types of stories of what was taking place in the South after Martin Luther King's assassination. Events were being broadcast on the TV, now allowing people to see the injustices as they were happening to Blacks in the South. Birmingham was the bedrock of synthetic integration. In 1963, Blacks were seen on TV being hosed down by police and attacked by police dogs. Bill Conner was the mayor of Birmingham, and he was campaigning. He had control of the police department and was enforcing these attacks upon the protestors to gain political advantage with the white voters.

Everyone saw kids being beaten after they joined the MLK group. I shed many tears over this. Some of my classmates who were still living in Alabama were able to be a part of the march and fight for equality in the South. How I wished that I had been able to be in the march with them. I realized that everybody had a part to play, and at that time my part was in finishing school. This motivated me to work harder toward being a success in my chosen field.

Today when I visit my hometown in Birmingham, Alabama, I make it a point to visit the Birmingham Civil Rights Institute. This is a large museum and research center that depicts the struggles of the Civil Rights Movement in the 1950s and 1960s. This always reminds me how far we as a race have truly come and how much further we have to go.

# Chapter 8

# THE DREAM

## *The Beginning*

With my newfound freedom and manhood, I began to explore this big world that I had much to learn about, beginning with my social life. Now that I was on my own, I was able to go to those places that I did not have the opportunities to go to when I was living at home with my parents. I attended parties and other social gatherings in my spare time. This allowed me to meet many new people and make a lot of new friends. At one of the parties that I attended, I met a young man who went by the name of Diddybow. Diddybow's real name was Arthur Humphry. Diddybow and I clicked right away and became good friends. Diddybow was a lot of fun to hang around with. We attended several night clubs together. Sometimes we would go from a one night club to the other.

Diddybow was a short, muscular, and well-built dude. He stayed dressed up and clean cut. His claim to fame was that he was a lady's man. One day while hanging out together, he introduced me to one of his cousins by the name of Benetta. Benetta and I went out on a double date with Diddybow and one of his girlfriends. Benetta and I hit it off, and this became the beginning of our courtship.

Benetta was a senior in high school at the time. Benetta was really a very beautiful young lady, you might say a diamond in the rough, so to speak. She enjoyed my company, and I enjoyed hers as well. Benetta came from a large family, and her family struggled financially as well. This was something that I understood and could relate to. Unfortunately, her family's economic situation seemed to have a harder effect on the children in her family. Benetta and her siblings were teased on many occasions at school for not having good-enough clothes to wear to school, and the children were very cruel to her and her siblings growing up.

Over time, Benetta and I began seeing more and more of each other, and the relationship got pretty serious. When I could, I would assist Benetta with buying new clothes for school. With new clothes, it was not too long before many of those little boys who teased her in school began to want to date her. But Benetta never forgot the cruelty of their words and how it made her and her siblings feel. She never gave those other fellows the time of day. I guess you could say I had this to my favor.

Benetta and I dated for about a year before I asked her father for her hand in marriage. We got married a few weeks after that. Nathaniel, a very good friend of mine stood in as my best man. We got married in a small house, in a small ceremony with a few family members and friends. At the time that we married, I was still living in my room at Ms. Moody's house, so Benetta moved in with me. Ms. Moody did not approve of me dating Benetta, let alone our getting married. She was very upset when I moved Benetta into my one-room quarters.

Benetta and Ms. Moody could not get along with one another for anything, and Benetta felt as if Ms. Moody had a mean demeanor and said she was just flat-out mean to her. She saw Ms. Moody as always having her nose in the air and was looking down at her every time they were around each other. Ms. Moody had heard rumors of social workers having to repeatedly come to her parents' home and that the living conditions in their home were deplorable. She assisted in the spreading of these rumors without considering the possibility that the so-called rumors were not true. The rumors were not true. The truth of the matter was that she didn't know much about their family at all. Her spreading these rumors was a sure indication of how much she disliked their family. The fact that she would be a part of such viciousness also revealed that she was not a true Christian.

One day Benetta cooked some chitterlings in Ms. Moody's kitchen, and Ms. Moody was not happy that Benetta had cooked anything in her kitchen and slapped her. Benetta was upset, but she did not hit her back. She realized Ms. Moody was very old, and if she had hit her, she could have caused her serious harm. Yet a pretty intense argument broke out as a result. I knew at that point it was time for us to find our place sooner than later. Shortly after that incident, we got word from Mrs. Hazel Carter that there was a duplex home for rent three doors down from their home. As soon as the opportunity presented itself, we moved out of Ms. Moody's home and into that small duplex apartment.

The apartment did not look like much initially. But Benetta and I fixed the apartment up real nicely. We painted the place up essentially and brought some nice furniture to go in it. By the time we had finished, the apartment looked immaculate. We were proud of how it turned out. When the landlord saw how nice we had fixed things up, she tried to increase the rent. I was not having that. We had an agreement. She expected me to stick to my part of the agreement, and I expected her to stick with her agreement, and we both did just that.

At this time Benetta was pregnant with our oldest daughter and before we knew it, our daughter had arrived. We named her La Grieta, after my older sister. She was a pretty little chocolate bundle. Not long after Lagrieta was born, my little brother moved into our duplex apartment with us. Freddie was also accepted into the medical technology school at Mercy Hospital. Freddie was to stay with us temporarily until he was able to afford his place. Needless to say, it was sort of tight with all three of us in this two-bedroom apartment. But we managed to work it out for a while. We lived in that apartment for about two years before I decided it was time to put some roots elsewhere.

During this time, black people were experiencing discrimination when it came to purchasing homes. Some homeowners refused to sell their residence to a black person. There were landlords in Ohio, who often refused to rent apartments or homes to a black person. The State of Ohio sought to eliminate segregation and discrimination in housing. To help end discrimination in this area, the Ohio Fair Housing Act was enacted in 1965. This legislation prohibited racial discrimination in housing except if the owner also resided in the building or if the home or apartment building had only one or two rental units. But this legislation did not end discrimination in housing. What it did do was to provide African Americans in Ohio with a legal means to secure equal access to housing.

In 1965, Ohio became one of the first states to enact fair housing legislation. In 1968 The House of Representatives passed the Fair Housing Act, known as the Civil Rights Act. This prohibited discrimination in the sale or rental of housing nationwide.

I remembered taking those trips to Mountain Brook to caddy and the nice homes that we would pass up in those mountains. I didn't' think I would be able to afford homes as nice as those, but I knew I wanted some of the things that I saw back then for me as an adult. I discovered later in life that where you live can have a significant effect on other parts of your life.

When Benetta and I started looking for a house, we began looking at some of the neighborhoods where mostly white people lived. Though Springfield was not segregated, it had neighborhoods that were considered black neighborhoods. Most blacks lived in the southwest part of the town. Many white people were known for residing in the extreme south part of Springfield or the north side of Springfield. To my knowledge, no blacks at that time lived south of Johns street.

After our real estate agent found out how much money I made, he was very impressed. He informed us that I qualified for a bigger home than we had originally anticipated purchasing. My income was very favorable, which it should have been. My normal work week as a night tech was sixty hours per week. The agent started showing us houses in the white neighborhoods. We heard about this split-level house in the Southgate area. It was located in an area where only whites or very few blacks were living at the time. Benetta and I went to check out the house.

We were excited to see the real estate agent at the showing. We viewed the house, and both Benetta and I liked the home. It was just as nice on the inside as it was on the outside. This house was located on the corner of Corlington Drive. It had a basement, three or four bedrooms, and a family room. There was a brick veneer with vinyl siding and a one-car attached garage. In the back of the house, there was a partial fence around the home. It was a beautiful home. We purchased the home and moved in a few weeks later.

This was a happy ending for us, but not many other black people at that time had experienced the same happy ending when purchasing a home in Springfield or in the State of Ohio. This moved me to write to the editor of the newspaper in Springfield about how I felt about the unfair housing in Ohio that was occurring at that time. The article was printed in the editorial section of the newspaper.

# FAIR HOUSING

To the Editor of The News:

Mrs. Helen R. Bowen's impression of her Negro friends and their feelings toward fair housing struck me as being bold, and if I might add, quite unique. It lends weight to the thesis often reiterated among Negroes: "White America under-stands very little about Negro feelings and aspirations." I, as a Negro, have heard implications of this sort many times, and occasionally have discussed the merits of this line of thought.

Through the grace of God, Mrs. Bowen, your Negro friends manage to speak to you at work, nothing else would be more decent and proper. Occasionally you might exchange points of view on the Vietnam War, air and water pollution, our rising crime rate, and any other subject that might crop up. After all, it helps to unleash those pent-up emotions that we as homo sapiens of the 20th century often encounter difficulty in concealing.

But yet and still, the question unfolds: Does this give your casual on-the-job acquaintance certification as a valid anal-ysis of our feelings toward fair housing? I feel that an apology is urgently needed if by chance you were misled into thinking that Negros in Springfield are not interested in acquiring decent homes, wherever the opportunity arises, whenever their monetary means and social status sanction such acqui-sition. Might I start apologizing now if my Negro brothers aided and abetted you in gathering this impression.

Just because the Negros of Springfield remain open-minded and are not up in arms over the issue, as is the case in Louisville, Kentucky, does not mean that they aren't con-cerned about it. As exponents of patience, we carry our pent-up hopes and wait. We try to discipline painful frus-trations through prayer, hoping that our white brothers will also discipline their emotions and aid in eventually making

Springfield a better place to work, worship, and live. Taking a moral stand for that reason is not too much to ask, is it?

Ms. Bowen, my people work alongside you and are presently taking part in defending this big hunk of land for you; and some are, as you have noted, good friends of yours. Then, why can't these good friends who work with you be given an opportunity to purchase a comfortable home wherever they please—even next door to you? Oops, pardon me! That's too much to ask from a good friend, or is it?

S. MORRIS HOLLOWAY

## *Home Sweet Home*

Despite being the only black family in the neighborhood, Benetta and I felt fairly comfortable living in the house on Corlington. We didn't have any interactions or run-ins with our neighbors; however, there was a white man who lived across the street, who kept staring over at our house from time to time. He was sort of creepy. He was one of the neighbors that we called briar hoppers. They were from Kentucky and Tennessee. They migrated to the North and brought along all of their prejudice with them.

One day, while I was outside tending to our yard, his son came over to speak to me. He told me that his father did not like the idea of black people living across the street from him, and he was going to move. The young man said that he could not understand why his father would say something like that since he went to high school with many black kids every day, and he could not understand the problem. Over time, his son and I became good friends. His dad eventually softened up over the years, and we were able to have some reasonable conversations with one another. Larry Z. told me that his father was very *impressed* with how we kept up the home. He even invited us over for dinner saying, *"We may have only beans," but y'all are welcome to share dinner with us."* I thanked him, but we never accepted the offer. I never had the time to socialize with him.

Shortly after we moved into the house on Corlington, Benetta and I had our second daughter. We thought she was going to be a boy and had planned to name him Morris Jr., but we had another girl, so we tried to find a name that would be close to mine. We named her Morine. Benetta said that this was going to be the last one. She wanted to pursue her career in nursing, and I was fine with that. I never got a boy, but we had two girls, and I believe that we were both happy about that. I would have liked to have a son, but it was not that high on my list of priorities.

Some of Benetta's old classmates and family would drive by the house and wonder how we got that house. They did not believe that we would be able to afford such a house. Many of Benetta's so-called friends had become very jealous and made snide remarks, saying that she would not be able to tend to the upkeep of the house. But we did and for several years our house was one of the nicest-looking homes on the block.

One summer, Benetta and I threw a cookout at the house and all of her family came over to the house. Some of our friends and a few of her siblings, cousins, aunts, and uncles showed up. They were impressed with what Benetta and I had accomplished. I overheard one of Benetta's uncles, called AB, and her dad, who they called Mack, talking about me. Mack said yes, "Benetta got a good one; he's really smart." And that was how I was able to afford our home. In 1968, it was very unusual for a black family to be able to afford a split-level house, if any house at all.

I was very ambitious, and I wanted to achieve a whole lot more. I felt like there would be more good things for us in the future. I saw this as only being the beginning.

## The Real Estate Broker

Because of my ambitions, I was also considered somewhat of a freak. There were not many black young men my age talking about doing the things that I talked about doing. I had big dreams of becoming a real estate agent and owning lots of rental real estate units that I would rent out to black and white tenants. At this time, real estate agents were known as real estate salespeople. To be a real estate salesperson, you had to be licensed by the state. The state issued the real estate test and upon passing the test, you were issued your real estate license. Then the licensed real estate salesperson was assigned to the real estate broker of their choice. Once a real estate broker was selected, they were required to display their license in the real estate broker's office where they worked.

I studied the primer book, took the test given by the state, and passed the test in 1970. After passing the real estate license exam, I could not just go out and sell property independently. Agents had to work under the scrutiny of the real estate broker for at least a year. I was informed that as a black agent that I was expected to work with a black broker. That same year, I was introduced to the first black real estate broker in Springfield by the name of Ralph Woodford. I worked under the direction of Ralph Woodford at his company, Zephr Hill Real Estate. He appeared to be a successful broker.

I worked part-time as an agent with a long-term goal of eventually purchasing rental properties and renting them out for a profit. I had set in my mind that eventually, when Benetta was able to attend nursing school and get her degree, that we could work together and purchase properties. The one issue I ran into was that many people at that time put more trust in the white real estate agent and patronized the white agents over the black agents. There were not a lot of black families who would trust a black real estate agent to sell their homes. It was more difficult for the black real estate agents to earn the trust of the clients, period. The black agents had to work twice as hard as the white agents did to make a sale.

Ralph Woodford owned many single-family houses and felt that it was time to expand his holdings. He was able to secure a federal loan to start the construction of a multiple-unit complex. He was working on what they called the Woodford project, and an unfortunate development took place during this project. The contractor who was hired took money from the Woodford project and used those funds on another project he was working on. This came to light after the federal authorities accused Ralph of misusing funds that were allocated to the Woodford project.

Ralph had hired an out-of-town contractor. It was discovered later that the contractor was not bonded. Ralph's attorney was responsible for verifying the building contractor's credentials and making sure that the contractor was bonded before they hired him. But his attorney, who was hired cheap, could best be described as a bootleg attorney, and what some might call a street attorney from right off the street corner. Obviously, he did not know much about real estate matters.

Since the contractor was not bonded, the only recourse for the federal government was to foreclose the Woodford project. And that's exactly what happened. Ralph lost the Woodford project and the Feds repossessed the property. After the government foreclosed on the property, Ralph lost everything. The word was that he was being punished for being so mean to other blacks and cheating them out of their properties over the years.

Another disgrace for the bootleg attorney came with an accusation that he had not paid his taxes for several years. At this point, he decided to pack up and move to Chicago with a beauty queen contestant. I never heard anything again about him after that.

I was able to maintain my real estate license and I eventually transferred to another real estate broker in Springfield. As time passed, there were multiple black brokers agents to choose from.

---

## Best Friends

---

It was the year 1964 when I met my good friend Nathaniel Radford. I met Nathaniel one day while shopping at one of the men's clothing stores downtown. I went into The Boston Store to purchase some items, and Nathaniel was working there as a store associate. While I was looking for some clothing articles, Nathaniel came to assist me, and we introduced ourselves to each other. I noticed his deep southern accent right away. It felt a little like home away from home. He told me he was raised in Leeds, Alabama. This is a small town close to Birmingham. He also said that he had recently dropped out of college. We continued to talk and reminisce about the South when I found out that he had attended Knoxville College, the same college my sister Marcia had attended. As always, God was moving and sending forth those godly connections.

Once he found out I had a car, we started going out to clubs and hanging out. We had a lot of fun every time we got together. It wasn't long after this that we became best friends. We were inseparable. Nathaniel was very articulate and had a very pleasant personality. He had a full head of curly hair that the women loved. He was a tall, brown-skinned man, well built, and a very neat dresser. He was known as a lady's man and rightly so because he dated a lot of women.

I always knew when I saw him, I could count on at least two things. Number one, he would come talking about politics, and number two, he would come with one of his lady friends. We could talk for hours about nothing and then a little bit of everything. Our most interesting conversations stemmed from politics and other current events. We both talked about positive events, and we normally agreed with one another. We seemed to have the same philosophy about life and were always able to support each other. Nathaniel was a positive man, and I did my best to stay around positive people.

The only thing wrong with Nathaniel was that he did not play golf. If he had been a golf player, we would have spent even more time together. We did find another thing in common, though, that allowed us to spend more time together. Nathaniel was continuing his education, and he suggested that I continue my education with him. So I enrolled in some classes with Nathaniel at Urbana College in Urbana, Ohio.

When I first met Nathaniel, he did not have a driver's license. I taught Nathaniel how to drive a car. He eventually got his license and shortly after bought himself an Oldsmobile Toronado. We arranged to commute together to college. We did that for two years. The only class I found interesting while attending Urbana College was the writing class that I took. I received an associate degree in liberal arts from The Urbana University College in 1977.

When Benetta and I married, Nathaniel stood as my best man. But Nathaniel himself was never a family man. For the time that I knew Nathaniel, he never married. He liked being a bachelor. He continued to be a lady's man throughout our acquaintance. After Benetta and I married, Benetta wanted us to double date with Nathaniel and his girlfriends. So Benetta and I and whomever Nathaniel was dating at that time would go out together to the clubs on the weekends and have a nice time.

Over time I began putting more focus on real estate. Along with real estate, working night shifts as a tech, and playing golf, Nathaniel and I began to spend less time together and have less in common. Nathaniel and I were good friends for many years. Eventually, he and I lost contact with one another. I have not spoken to him for years, but I have thought about him from time to time.

---

## The Intruder

---

One night, Benetta and the kids were at home while I was working the night shift at the hospital. Benetta heard what sounded like glass breaking. She immediately called me at the hospital and told me that she thought someone was breaking into the basement. She tiptoed and heard what sounded like someone moving around in the basement. She got close enough to the steps so that I could hear the glass continuing to break while she was talking to me on the phone.

She hollered down the steps "Is anyone down there?" When no one answered, she went back up the hall and into our bedroom, got the gun, and then went into the girls' room, got them up out of their bed, brought them into our bedroom, and locked the door.

I told Benetta to call the police. Our neighbor was a cop who worked for the sheriff's department, and he overheard the call when it came in on his police scanner. He came over to the backyard of our house and threw a couple of rocks at our bedroom window to get Benetta's attention. When Benetta saw that it was him outside, she went to the window, and he told her to throw him down the keys to the front door. She threw the keys down to him, and he came into the front door armed with his gun, and he went down into the basement.

To his surprise, he found a young boy lying on the basement floor knocked out drunk. He had broken the basement window and came in. It was Martha Lee's nephew, Stevie. Martha Lee was a church friend, who lived about a block up from our house. Stevie had babysat the girls sometime before. He was only around sixteen or seventeen years of age. We figured he was probably confused since he was so drunk and didn't realize where he was. Thinking he was at his home, he broke the window and entered the house. It was winter, so he was probably trying to get out of the cold.

The local police eventually showed up, and I arrived shortly after they came on the scene. They took the young boy downtown, and we were not sure what happened to him after that. I was glad that Benetta and the kids were fine, and everybody was safe and sound.

# Chapter 9
# AGAINST THE ODDS

---

## *The TURF Club*

---

I continued to work sixty hours a week as a night tech, while playing golf in my spare time. Golf continued to be my passion, and I practiced golfing every chance that I could. If I could have, I would have practiced my golf swing every day, but with the other responsibilities that I had, I was unable to do that.

In Ohio, I found that playing on a golf course was child's play compared to when I had been playing on those dirt fields for all those years. In 1968, I began to seriously think about playing competitive golf. It was at this time that Mr. Carter introduced me to the Turf Club. This was an all-black golf club. We met on the weekends and played on Saturdays and Sundays. I dominated in winning the Turf Club championship titles throughout the 1970s and 1980s. These competitions prepared me for higher-level games to come.

I met a lot of influential people at the Turf Club. Brook Laurence joined the Turf Club after retiring from the Cincinnati Reds pitching staff alongside his brother Milt Laurence. Brooks was the first black player to garner celebrity status with the Cincinnati Reds. His nickname was the "Bull" because of his durability as a relief pitcher. He would return to the mound and win games on short notice. One day we were conversing, and he gave me some advice in regard to golfing. He said, "Morris, you need to block out all the crowds when you're out there." Of course, I took his advice.

During one of our Turf meetings, to our surprise, he brought in two very well-known Cincinnati Reds baseball players to one of the golf outings and introduced us to them. Their names were Joe Black and Kenny H Griffin Jr. Joe had retired from baseball at this time, but Kenny was a current Reds superstar. When Kenny's fans saw him on the golf course, he would oblige them with an autograph before returning to his golf game. Kenny saw me playing golf one day and after finishing our round and waiting for the final group to come off the golf course, he came up to me with a puzzled look on his face. Then he asked me, "How can a "little man" like you hit a golf ball so far as 300-plus yards?"

I just laughed for a moment. Then I told him, "My power comes from a full shoulder turn, a restricted lower body turn, and a good cock and uncock of the wrist." I then went on to tell him how impressed I was when I see someone like him have the ability to hit a baseball out of the park. We both got in a good laugh, as we shared our admiration for each other's abilities.

**All The Way Through**

When Morris Holloway hits one off the tee, he puts his
everything behind the drive, as shown in this picture. Note the
follow-through of Holloway, blasting off No. 15 tee.

Morris Holloway in full swing!
The City Amateur Golf Tournament

I continued practicing my swing every day, trying to perfect my golf
swings. I worked on those things that I felt needed to be corrected. My
frame of thought was always in correction, control, concentration, and
consistency. I had a practice routine, and I stuck with it.

## Springfield
## City Amateur Golf Competition
## (1970)

I n 1970, I entered my first Springfield City Amateur Golf Tournament competition. I did not have high expectations entering this tournament. This was a trial balloon for me. I just wanted to see how I would fare against white players. In the first round, I was very competitive. I was at the top of the field with several other golfers. During the second round, I continued to play pretty well, and I continued to score close to par golf. Once again, I was one of the top four players in the tournament. At this point, the city amateur golf title could be headed in one of four directions, Butch Macbeth, Paul Flora, me, or the defending champion, John Carper.

In the third round, I wasn't entirely on my "A" game and posted a 76, 4 over par. The newspaper described this round as being "the round that I skied into a 76." The 76 was not a terrible round, but it was an unusually high score for me.

No one knew that I was nursing a cold with a high temperature, and I didn't want to use that as an excuse for my performance. So I continued and pushed past how I was feeling. That evening, I medicated myself and drank lots of water and fluids overnight. This did the trick, and by morning, I felt a hundred percent better and was ready for the final round to commence.

On the back nine, four players had a realistic chance of winning this tournament. I moved ahead, and by the 17th hole, I realized that I had a one-shot lead over my closest competitor, Butch Macbeth. In realizing this, I tried to keep my focus on my golf game. I tried not to look at the dark clouds forming overhead.

The four players in my group moved to the last tee, the 18th hole. This is when we started to feel a few sprinkles of rain on our tee shots and moved down the fairway. We were all hoping to finish playing before the rain came down harder, but just as we were preparing our shots to the final green, heavy drops of rain began falling.

All three of the other players had hit their second shots. We all started popping up our umbrellas to beat off the rain. I chose a club in preparation to hit my second shot when all of a sudden, a stop play alarm went off, and play was suspended. None of us golfers knew what was going on. There we were in the middle of the fairway with pelts of rain coming down on us, waiting to finish the play.

Ben Johnson, a black golfer, had been following my group and was curious about my predicament. Ben knew USGA golf rules. He knew that no golf tournament should be stopped unless there was lightning in the area. Ben hurried to the pro shop and confronted Joe Lodermier, the Pro responsible for sounding the stop play alarm, and he asked Joe, "Why do you stop the tournament when no lightning had been seen?" Joe responded, "I'm just trying to give everyone a chance." "Bull****, Joe, you are wrong!" He said, "Morris is standing out there under a tree in the pouring rain waiting to hit his shot. There isn't any lightning in the sky, so the tournament should be finished right now!"

After Ben finished with Joe, within just a few moments, the resume play horn went off, and the tournament resumed. By this time, the golf course was saturated with rain. I was anxious to finish playing. I knew that this was a pivotal shot. I hit a low hook shot below the tree that ended up hole-high in the greenside sand trap. I blasted out to about seven feet, leaving myself a reasonable putt for par. And then, I missed the putt.

Butch Macbeth's next shot would be what they called "the miracle shot" and would become the talk of the town. While a torrent of rain was still falling from the sky, Butch hit a five-iron shot over a group of trees. The ball made a splash as it hit the green and stopped eight feet from the hole. Butch rolled the ball on the line and the ball splashed to the hole. When the ball disappeared into the hole, I knew that the game was over. This was a game shot. There would be no playoff. My hopes were dashed in that final hole. A two-shot swing had taken place. My bogie 5 on the hole and Butch's birdie 3 made the difference.

I left the tournament that day looking forward to the next chance that I would have to win this prestigious event. One thing was for sure, I had given the City of Springfield a new name to talk about and a sports event that everyone would remember for some time to come. The next day, the *Springfield News-Sun* newspaper had our pictures displayed in the newspaper, stating a local celebrity was born! I welcomed the gesture.

The newspaper printed about how Macbeth came from-behind on that final hole and how he finished up the winner with a 290, just a stroke ahead of me. Of course, I came in second place. Bob Horton won the junior championship, and Mar Ginaven was a senior champ that day. I shook Butch's hand in congratulations for winning the tournament. Little did they know my quest to win in this competition had just begun. This was the springboard for my participation in other golf tournaments. No black golfer had ever achieved this by coming so close to winning the local Springfield City Amateur golf tournament. I didn't realize the importance of this tournament until after it was all over.

# The First Time Ever!

Congratulations To Victor

Morris Holloway, left, can still smile as he congratulates Butch MacBeth for his come-from-behind victory on the final hole Sunday in the City Amateur Golf Tournament at Snyder Park. MacBeth sank a 15-foot putt for his one-stroke victory. That's Tom Schenher, center, watching the exchange.

1970 Springfield City Amateur Golf Competition
(1st Time Runner-up)

Often, I would reminisce on the fact that if I had gained one stroke, I could have been the champion that day. This made me practice even harder and take the game more seriously because I knew that I was in fact a true competitor in the sport of golf. I was able to win, and I would return.

### *The Springfield Championship League*

In the year 1970, I got my first real exposure to competitive golf. It all began to take shape after I was introduced to a white man named Russ Hemry. Russ was a well-known golfer in Springfield. He was also the founder of the Springfield Championship League. He told me that he had heard about me through some friends, and he came out to see if what he had heard was true. After watching me play, he said he was impressed, and he wanted me to join the league. This league would allow me to compete against the best golfers in Springfield. I accepted right away. Only Springfield's best golfers were offered the opportunity to be a part of this league. They played golf the way it was supposed to be played. If I was to become a member of this team, this would mean I would be competing in a two-man team event. I was excited about this format.

My first competition with the league was in 1970 when I partnered with Tom Sheridan. I felt like it was a great experience; we played well together, and we came in first place in this Springfield Championship League competition. We received an engraved trophy with a $500.00 bonus. It also gave us some exposure in the newspaper, and my picture was once again posted in the newspaper. And, the league presented me with the reward of being "The most improved player of the year."

My second competition with the league was in 1971. This time I partnered with Dave Mattes. Dave was a local attorney. He was a pleasant person to be around and had what we called a "sweet golf swing." Dave and I won first prize in this Springfield Champion League competition again. Again, the event was covered in the newspaper, and I gained local notoriety. We celebrated with a dinner affair that was held at the Springfield Country Club. There were approximately 100 guests at this event. It was a big deal and a great honor.

I became noticed as a worthy opponent. Who would have thought that this black boy from the South, who started out golfing in the dirt field and cow pastures in Alabama using secondhand iron clubs and a tin cup for a hole would compete against men who had the advantage of playing on a real golf course? And who knew I would be thought of as the competitor that came to town and turned local golf upside down. No one, but it happened.

.F CHAMPS—Winners of the Championship G
eid Park are Morris Holloway, left, and Tom S
ss Jewelry. Wayne Tillman and Bob Ross, Sr
ole loop tourney with a 141 total.

1970 The Springfield championship league
(1st win)

Regardless of how good a golf player that I had become, it didn't tear down the walls of prejudice that had been put up to keep blacks from moving ahead in this sport. Russ Hemby, the founder of the Springfield championship league, had the authority to send a golfer from the Springfield district to the Ohio State Amateur Tournament competition. He was to make the final determination. The top players were generally the ones selected to compete. Russ Hemry chose a white player over me to compete in this tournament.

It was a known fact that I was at the top of my game and that I was a public link golfer. Yet I was denied the opportunity when he selected a white player. He was a good player, but he did not have the notoriety or the experience and exposure that I had in the game. My fellow white golfers informed me that no black players had ever participated in the Ohio Amateur State Tournament. It was apparent that no black players were allowed to participate as long as their selection process was in place.

I was upset, but there was nothing that I could do about it. I had to fight the forces of racism in other ways. I realized that even when I was playing some of my best golf that I stood the chance of being overlooked and denied the opportunity to compete because of the color of my skin. It would have been an honor to be able to compete in this event. To excuse Russ's decision in selecting a white golfer, I was told this was a very prestigious event and part of the deciding factor as to who would be selected to attend this event was based on eligibility and only country club amateur golfers were eligible to compete. Naturally, I did not belong to a country club. I was determined not to let this deter me from continuing to compete in other competitive events.

The league eventually folded when Russ Henry became ill a few years later. He was a heavy smoker and was diagnosed with COPD. He retired due to health concerns.

## *The Controversy, The Second Time Around*

In 1973, I entered Springfield's City Amateur Golf Competition for the second time. This ended up being what they called a controversial event. The leader started with a 9-shot lead in the final round. This put him well ahead of the other competitors. The eyes of the crowd would be on this player from the third round clear up to the end of the tournament. No one anticipated this player losing the tournament with what seemed like an insurmountable lead. The pressure was on because the eyes of the gallery would be on him following his every shot.

We figured the leader must have wanted to win this prestigious event the way that he started. Nonetheless, I felt that if I played my game well, anything was possible. Even if I did not overcome this lead, I would be able to appreciate another second-place finish. As we moved to the final 9 holes the big lead shrunk. Our leader was what we golfers called 'leaking oil" at 6 over par. I was at even par. Only 3 shots separated me from the leader as he approached the difficult 15th hole. He parred the 15th hole and then boogied the 16th hole, leaving him with a 2-shot lead going into the final 18th hole.

I stepped up to the tee, took my shot, and finished my round a hole ahead, posting a one-over-par 73. As the crowd followed the tournament leader, they wondered if he could hold on to this lead. All he needed to keep the lead was to finish with a bogey 5 on the final hole. He did exactly that. In summary, he shot a tournament-high score of 81 and earned a one-shot victory. I was certain that if we had not run out of holes, I would have overcome his lead and earned the title that day.

This event revealed that Ron Slick may have lied about his score during the 3rd round. Ron was known for having a hole in his pocket. No one could attest to his putting out since his playing partners were said to have been searching for a lost ball at that time. Even though the other players had their doubts, nothing could be done unless the infraction was called "on the golf course" at the time it may have occurred. This was a USGA rule.

Once again, I congratulated my opponent and moved on to the next event. Both my and Slick's pictures were posted in the local newspaper, along with the junior and senior division winners. The newspaper also printed a picture of him receiving a congratulations kiss from his mother, Mrs. Robert Slick, after winning. The newspaper stated that Ron Slick held off the last round surge by Morris Holloway to take a 1-stroke victory. So what happened? I guess nobody but Ron Slick knows what really happened, and of course God.

The 1973 Springfield City Amateur Tournament. Many golfers seemed impressed with my close call to victory.

I performed the best that I could, and I knew I had nothing to be ashamed of. Once again second place, becoming better known as "the bridesmaid but never the bride." I continued in my quest to take the first-place prize. Over a -year period, I continued to challenge amateur golfers for titles. I began participating in other competitions and events in Springfield, such as the Clark County Match Play Tournaments. In 1974 I came in second place in the Clark County Match Play Tournament

---

## The Match

---

In 1976 I competed in the Clark County Match Play tournament. My match ended up being a dramatic one. I was three holes ahead of my opponent going into the last three holes when we had reached the semifinal stage of the event. Four players were left. I had my opponent "Domie"—*I was 3 up and 3 to go*. I never thought about losing this match.

My opponent birdied the 16th and 17th holes. This put me at 1 hole ahead going to the final hole. Normally, this type of pressure would not bother me—if it had not been for the fact that the last shot I hit was the world's worst golf shot. I hit the ball, and it ended up stymied behind a tree. I could not believe it. I bogeyed the hole. My opponent sensed an opening as he stepped up to tee. He hit the ball on the green and parred the hole and to my shock and dismay, I was headed for a playoff.

This led to a sudden-death playoff. We went to the first tee and started over. I lost the first hole of the playoff, and the only thing left for me to do was to compete for third place against another golfer. I congratulated my opponent Dave on his win as he went on to compete for first place. I finished in third place, and I never forgot this humiliating defeat. This caused me to practice even more, still hearing those unforgettable words of Mr. Carter's reverberate through my mind to "Never give up." And I continued.

## *Golf Competitions (1970–1976)*

In 1976, I placed first in the Mercy Hospital Championship. In 1977, I was the winner in the Jim Foreman Classic Tournament at Snyder Park Golf Club (posting par golf of 144 for two days of play). Between 1970 and 1975, I was runner up in both Reid Park Golf Club and Snyder Park Golf Club Championship events. In 1975, at the Ohio State Public Golfers Tournament held in Mt. Vernon, I posted an opening round of 66 (6 under par). The tournament sponsors and the news reporters were excited about the prospect of a black golfer winning this classic event. I went on to finish in the top five positions. Some of Ohio's top public golfers competed in this competition. And in 1976, in Cleveland, Ohio, at the Ohio State Public Golfers tournament, I posted the first recorded hole-in-one shot at the Highland Park Golf course.

## *Local Four Set for US Open Qualifier*

El Collins, the PGA professional at Reid Park Golf Club took notice of my golfing talent. Since he was in good golfing standing with the USGA, he wanted to sponsor me to try out for the US Open. Only low-handicap amateur golfers could enter into the regional US Open qualifiers. He entered my name, along with a couple of other amateur players by the name of Keith Hughes and Roy Richards. Just being able to participate in a US open qualifier was a big deal.

The regional qualifiers took place at Markatewa Golf Club This was a country club in Cincinnati, Ohio. El drove the three of us to Cincinnati for a practice round. It was a beautiful golf setting. The golf course presented a worthy challenge, with its lush, sloped fairways and magnificent sloped greens. On the day we were to compete, the sky was overcast with thick gray and black clouds. Nevertheless, we were told that unless there was lightning, we had to tee it up and play. The rain came down pretty heavy that day. As we stood on the first tee, the torrential rain was blinding. We could hardly see the fairway ahead. Soon we all noticed the significant drop in the temperature as the drops of rain continued to pour down on the course.

I was hoping that the play could get canceled, but since there was no lightning, the tournament officials insisted that we *"play golf."* We all played very poorly that day. I made up in my mind that I would never again attempt to play golf under such conditions. This would not be my last attempt. I went to the open qualifier twice.

El and I became close friends since I stayed in the limelight in local golf tournaments. He was no stranger to black golfers since he had befriended Pete Brown and the legendary Charlie Gifford. When the City Commissioners decided to close the Snyder Park Golf Club and eliminate the pro golf position at Reid Park, I was the only black golfer who stood up and testified on behalf of El Collins. I thought of El as a national treasure. He was a valuable asset for the City of Springfield.

No one stepped up to purchase the Reid Park Golf Club when the city manager decided to withdraw the city from the golf business. El

Collins and his son put in a winning bid. He would have an impact on local golf for years to come, much to my delight.

As much as I loved golf, my wife Benetta hated it. Benetta would tell people if I was not at work or home sleeping, I was golfing. Benetta said she was proud of me as a golfer; however, she never got involved in my golf activities. I'm not certain of this, but it always seemed like she felt as if she was competing with golf. It could also have been that golf took away her time with me. I remember her saying, at one time, "I don't like golf and don't understand why you want to buy old houses.' Benetta hated both of my ambitions. I told Benetta I planned to use the notoriety that I was receiving from playing golf to help us with purchasing homes and renting out properties. Yet, she couldn't see my vision. I wanted her to see the vision and pull with me. But she thought it was all foolishness. In the end, it was these differences that became some of the main factors in our drifting apart.

S. Morris Holloway tees off.

# Chapter 10
# MY SOUL LOOKS BACK

## *The Help!*

I continued to work the 10 p.m. to 8 a.m. shift as a night tech at the hospital. I worked this shift six days a week. All the techs seemed surprised that I stayed in this position as night tech for as long as I did. I held this position for several years. I ran into a lot of jealousy from my black coworkers who did not encourage me but would discourage me with every opportunity at work. After I was selected to be the night lab tech, I overheard one of the black techs conversing in the restroom. He was laughing because during one of our continuing education classes, he noticed I was nervous when I was giving my presentation.

It was early in my career, and I didn't have a lot of experience being in group settings. So he was right, I was a little nervous. After that, I was determined that I was going to be better prepared. So, I practiced at it until I became more confident at speaking in groups. I knew I belonged there. I just wanted to prove to my peers that I belonged there as well. Over time the demands in the lab had picked up. As things began to change in regard to technology and so forth; so did how we were to do some of the testings. For instance, the way the ER patient started getting basic testing done changed, including CBCs, urinalysis, blood sugar, BUN, creatinine, electrolytes, sodium, potassium, chloride, and $CO_2$. The cardiac testing eventually became another standard test ordered. Techs also began doing EKGs for patients coming in with chest pains. They did the blood testing and electrocardiogram (EKGs). The more things changed, the more work we had to do.

The blood tests were now being timed and periodic hemoglobin tests and coagulation (PTT) tests were being ordered 24/7, and we had to respond to ER test demands that continued to increase. It was more than evident that there was no way that one person could handle all these tasks alone anymore. I needed help.

## Little Brother

About this time, my brother Freddie completed his tech training at Mercy Hospital, and he was assigned to work the night shift with me. We worked the night shift alongside each other for several years. We both worked very hard; however, Freddie was not as dedicated as I was to the profession. At times, we issued up to thirty units of blood on trauma patients. Over the years Freddie and I saw all kinds of crazy things occur in the blood lab. These were things that the average person would not think could happen in a hospital. One particular crazy incident that comes to mind was the incident that took place with Dr. X. He had a patient that he said was in dire need of blood. Unfortunately, we didn't have any blood to give to Dr. X at the time that was compatible with his patient. We didn't like it any more than he did, but there was nothing we could do about it.

Nonetheless, this Dr. X demanded we give him some blood regardless of the type. In a rush to give blood to this trauma patient, Dr. X took some blood from the blood bank refrigerator. The units had not been cross-matched for the patient. He did this, even after we informed him that this was not a good idea since the blood was not a match. He insisted on giving the patient this blood. Not only did he insist on breaking protocol and taking the blood, but he also infused it. We found out later, the trauma patient died. This probably would have happened with or without the blood.

Then there was another incident that happened involving Dr. X. This time he demanded that we issue him FFP (fresh frozen plasma). Freddie and I informed him that we had to thaw the FFP in a 37° C incubator before he could give it to the patient. Any abrupt means of thawing the plasma could have catastrophic results. It had to be done this way to prevent the bags from bursting.

Dr. X insisted on taking the frozen FFP with him to the floor. After several conversations with this doctor, we finally issued him the FFP. He took the FFP to the floor and placed it in a microwave oven to thaw the plasma quicker. When he turned on the microwave oven to thaw the plasma quicker, The oven literally "exploded!" *It blew-up* due to the protein content of FFP, FFP should be thawed in 37-degree water and thaw very gently, employing a mechanical agitator. Heat would cause the plastic bags to burst, as it did, thus wasting the product. Needless to say, he had egg on his face. It was the most misguided event/episode that we had ever heard of. As far as we knew this Dr. X was never reprimanded for either of the incidents.

## The Case of the Stolen Golf Clubs

There was nothing that I liked better than getting together with a few buddies to play a round of golf. Several of my golf buddies and I would plan tee times and meet at the golf course on the weekends to play a round of golf. Afterward, we would all go over to the golf course restaurant and get something to eat. We left our golf clubs outside the front of the restaurant while we ate. This was a designated area for leaving golf bags while in the restaurant. We did this on several occasions and never thought anything of it.

One day after dining, we came out, I couldn't find my golf clubs. I looked around and sure enough, my golf clubs were gone. Everyone else's clubs were there, but mine were missing. We talked to people in the clubhouse, and no one at the clubhouse or pro shop knew what had happened to my golf clubs. It was obvious that my golf clubs had been stolen by a thief. I referred to the person at that time as being "low down."

I posted a $50 reward for any information leading to the recovery of my golf clubs. This became the beginning of an unbelievable "saga" to get my golf clubs back. I got a couple of tips from a couple of prominent golfers by the name of Jerry Carl and The golf pro El Collins. I was informed that a man in a vehicle had been seen checking out golf clubs in the back seat of his car. This person became my main suspect. Ironically El Collins, the golf pro at Reid Golf Club, remembered this young man who had accompanied two kids to the golf course. They had been seen around that area. As fate would have it, one of the kids with him that day had posted a hole in one. He registered the kids' name and address in the pro shop in anticipation of receiving an award for the hole in one from a golf club company.

Two days went by and still no word on my golf clubs. At this point, my brother Freddie and I turned Dick Tracy to solve this case. Freddie and I decided we would track down this man, using the kid's address from the pro shop. The kid lived out in the Huber Heights community, about twenty miles from Springfield. We found the house, and Freddie and I introduced ourselves to the kid's mother and explained to her my dilemma. She allowed us to wait for this guy at her home, being confident that we were mistaken. Meanwhile, we had a good conversation with the kid's mother, a wife of an Air Force colonel. She told us that the coach, Larry X (the culprit) was not the type who had to steal and how he was an only child who came from a good family.

That day he had taken two of her kids to Kitty Hawk to play golf. Larry X had made himself available when it came to transporting the children in the neighborhood to various links in the area. He was known for chaperoning the kids at local golf courses. While we were having this conversation, the coach pulled up in his vehicle with two of the kids that he chaperoned in the vehicle with him. Freddie and I went outside and approached his vehicle as he was pulling into the driveway. Right away, I saw my clubs and a pull-cart, all in the back seat of the station wagon.

When he saw us, a look of dismay came upon his face. He was shocked to see us. Freddie and I told Larry that the clubs that were in his back seat were mine. He tried to deny that the clubs were mine. In an attempt to disguise my clubs, he had put them in another bag. However, this was not a good enough disguise because I was still able to identify them as being my clubs. My three-wood had a chip in it. The golf clubs, golf balls, and the wristwatch that he had all had my name on them. They were beyond a fact—my clubs.

He then acted as if he was getting ready to get back in his vehicle and leave. My brother Freddie wasn't having that and told the guy to stop when he grabbed my three-wood club from the golf bag and told him that he would knock the \*\*\*\* out of him if he tried to leave. Larry continued to maintain his innocence. Remember this was the neighborhood's favorite son. By this time a group of the white neighborhood residents had gathered in front of this house and this man's vehicle. Freddie and I looked around, and we looked like two flies in a glass of milk. Tensions were building.

I insisted that the authorities be called so that we could get the matter sorted out. The kids' mother went inside and called the local sheriff's department. Once the sheriff showed up, Freddie and I informed the sheriff about my golf clubs being stolen at Reid Park and what led us to this boy's home. We pointed to the clubs in his vehicle and told him that they were mine. We also told him that all the items we spoke of in his car had my initials on them as proof that they were mine.

The sheriff had all of us follow him up the hill to the Huber Heights precinct so that he could sort through everything. As he pulled each item out of the bag, they all had my initials on them as I had told him. After examining the clubs, the deputy sheriff turned to him and said to the young white guy, "You sorry SOB, you have stolen this man's golf clubs." He also told him, "This is considered a felony." The golf clubs were worth more than 500 dollars.

The deputy sheriff asked me if I wanted to press charges. I didn't want to press charges because I knew if I did they would have to keep my clubs for evidence, which meant I would not be able to use them during my next golf competition, so I told him I didn't want to press charges. The fact that I had my golf clubs back was more than enough for me. I also told the deputy sheriff that parents of the children he was coaching or chaperoning should be notified of his behavior and of what he had been teaching their children. Obviously, he was teaching the kids to steal golf clubs. Thank goodness no damage had been done to my golf clubs. I could hardly wait to get back to my practice routine.

The story of Freddie's and my adventure spread throughout golf circles in Springfield. I received a call from a *Springfield News-Sun* sports writer who offered to print our story in the sports section. Freddie and I met with him and recounted in detail the whole saga of the lost and found golf clubs. I told the journalist who reported this story that this episode reminded me of a guy I knew from Birmingham. He had everything he needed, but he stole anyway. After being paroled from jail, while on his way home, he stole a car. This guy seemed very similar to that guy. Larry X had everything. He was an only son. He coached a little league team and was involved in all types of sports, and yet he goes and does something like this.

Benetta told the journalist that she was very happy that I was able to recover my golf clubs. According to her, "for a couple of days, he was a nasty individual, mean, and hard to live with." One thing was certain, I returned to Springfield a very happy young man.

## *Freddie's Adventure*

Freddie stayed with us until he met a young lady, and they became serious. After a brief courtship, they married. Freddie was an all-around man. Both he and his wife liked to party. It got to the point that Freddie was going out and partying all the time. People made jokes about how serious Nathaniel and I were "never having a good time" and how Freddie was the exact opposite.

Freddie was flashy. He had bought this nice, flashy car. He dressed in nice, flashy expensive clothes. He was known around town as "fast Freddie." For a while, he and his wife enjoyed the fast life, and they got along well. But soon they started having more disagreements. His marriage lasted about a year before the problems began to set in, and they parted ways. After the separation, Freddie moved back in with us.

I talked Freddie into purchasing a small house. I thought it would be a good thing for Freddie to own his property and hoped that it would settle him down a bit. After moving into his new house, Freddie met his soon-to-be next wife, Jacinta. This marriage lasted for two years before it fell apart as well. Jacinta became pregnant, and Freddie became a father as the marriage came to an end. After the second divorce, Freddy's nerves began bothering him, and he later suffered a nervous breakdown. While all this was taking place, he refused to let go of his fast lifestyle and continued hanging out with his buddies and women while trying to keep up with his work.

I tried to tell Freddie he could not do all these things and be successful. Eventually, he was going to have to make a choice, or a choice would be made for him. As expected, everything eventually caught up with Freddie and trying to live a fast life caused his health to deteriorate even more. My mother came to Springfield and escorted Freddie back to Alabama. I was put in charge of selling Freddie's house. I found a buyer, and that was the end of my brother's adventure in Ohio.

After Freddie returned to Alabama to recuperate, different techs were assigned to fill his position on the night shift. There were also many changes taking place at the hospital during this time. The Catholic influence at the hospital was slowly fading away. The sister who was running the hospital allowed a CEO from the private sector to assume leadership. This caused a dramatic change in the hospital, and it affected everyone in the hospital, especially me. Dr. Hunter abruptly announced that she would be retiring, and then Cass told me that she felt it was time for her to retire as well. She had a good run, and she was not happy with the changes that were taking place throughout the hospital. She finished her last days at the hospital, and all the techs wished her well as they gave their heartfelt goodbyes. This was truly the end of an era.

## *The Complaint*

After Cass and Dr. Hunter retired from the hospital, things were never the same. We obtained new lab management. The technology program at Mercy Hospital was transferred to Clark Technical College where they remained affiliated with Mercy Hospital and continued internships. I continued to work as a night tech for a few more years when the hospital changed our workweek to a forty-hour workweek. The new lab managers decided to appoint a white tech as a second- and third-shift supervisor. The tech was a veteran with a military background. Though he had the experience, he did not have the tenure that I had. I felt that I should have been considered first for the position.

I was very disappointed and frustrated about the situation. I had been working at the hospital for ten years, and for them to assign someone over me without considering me was like a slap in the face. Benetta encouraged me to seek justice. After much thought, I decided to take my case to the EEOC. I filed my complaint with the federal government and the Human Resource Department. I wrote a seven-page complaint, informing them that I had been successfully doing this job for ten years. The Human Resource Department conducted a study/audit and discovered that no minorities had ever been hired in a supervisory position. John Hush, a caseworker, represented me, and in time, the hospital was found guilty of discriminating against minorities.

Eventually, John Hush took over the personnel manager position at Mercy Hospital. The hospital was forced to establish supervisory positions for blacks in particular, throughout the entire hospital. A few years after the complaint was filed, I was presented with the opportunity to be a supervisor again. I accepted the position and was given the supervisory position for the second and third shifts. This was a salaried position. I discovered while working in this position that I had been making more money working as a bench tech. So I soon gave up the supervisory position where I could now work a regular shift and earn overtime pay when extra hours were available.

## The Little Black Baby

There were other racist incidents that took place throughout the hospital, such as the black baby incident. A black baby was admitted into the hospital on the night shift. The registered nurse who was helping the parents and monitoring the baby consulted with a pediatrician about the baby who was having seizures. The nurse was very concerned for the baby and feared for the baby's life. The pediatrician's response was, "That's a nigger baby; you can't kill a nigger baby," This was a white established pediatrician who made this racist remark. He was also a well-known staff doctor at the hospital, and in his lofty position, he considered himself to be untouchable. The RN, who happened to be black, reported the pediatrician, but the doctor was never disciplined for his behavior. The baby passed away overnight.

Part 3

# THE DREAM AND
# THE LEGACY

# Chapter 11
# THE DOMESTIC STORM

## *The Landing*

The only problem with flying is that eventually, you have to land. When it came time to land, I landed rather hard, if I might say so myself. In life, we all have to live and learn. Some of us have to learn more than others. Benetta and I soon found out that we both had much to learn about life and marriage. As Benetta's and my marriage continued to deteriorate, it seemed to me like Benettea was in search of something. I didn't understand at the time what it was that she was looking for. At one point, she became more involved in the church and became an inspiring missionary. The dictates of the church were very strict. She had to have a very modest appearance and was not allowed to wear any makeup, pants, or jewelry.

I never had an interest in becoming more involved in the church. I felt as if Benetta's main focus became the church. I think we were what the church calls unequally yoked. So, she began going her way and I began going mine. We started having a difference of opinion about us going out to the clubs. Despite how Benetta felt about it, I continued to go out to the clubs with my friends. This led to many other differences in the marriage.

It got to the point that we could hardly communicate without there being some sort of disagreement. Anytime I voiced concerns about how things could be improved with managing the house or kids, she would tell me she was a type "A" person, and I was a type "B" person, and that's why she had her way of doing things and why I had my way of doing things. There was never any compromise or place of agreement.

We argued over little things and had a lot of little misunderstandings, like checking my daughter's ears for ear wax before she sent her off to school or asking her to use a cutting board when cutting meat instead of cutting the meat on the unprotected counter. Every time I said something about any type of improvement in an area, she became upset. It became apparent to me that we had different ways of doing things as well as differences of opinion.

## *Family Vacations*

I tried to keep us together as a family and establish more connections by going on yearly family vacations. Benetta and I and the kids went on family vacations every year. I wanted my girls to see and experience visiting parts of the world that I never had the chance to see. So, every year, we would pack up and go. I would drive my car to save money for the trip. We traveled to places like St. Louis, Alabama, Niagara Falls, Canada, Miami, New York, and Florida.

One-year Benetta told me that she just wanted the two of us to go on vacation together. She said that she was at home with the kids all day, and she needed some time with just me and her, without the kids. She wanted the kids to stay with a babysitter. I had no idea what she was talking about. I wanted my girls to come with us. I told her if they didn't go with us, we weren't going and that was the end of that.

As much as Benetta and I had in common, we also had deep differences. Because I had lived in the South, especially in Birmingham, Alabama, I was aware of the prejudices out there against blacks and what was taking place at the time. Benetta however lived in Springfield, Ohio, all her life, and she had no idea about some of the prejudice and struggles that blacks were facing in other areas in the country. A lot of prejudice that took place in Springfield at this time was done undercover. She was unaware of all the cultural stigmas when it came to black and white people. As we traveled to the South, as we did on several occasions to places like Alabama, I had to show her how she should and should not act.

I was conscious of some of the dangers out there even then when traveling with the family. I would always take my gun with me and keep it stored under the seat for protection. Traveling as far as we were traveling at all hours and being a black family, we never knew who we might run into. On the flip side, we risked the police finding our "protection." I remember being pulled over by the police during one of our vacation trips and Benetta pushing my gun back further under my set so that it could not be seen by the officer. I knew we took a chance having it in the car, but at that time, I was more concerned about what might have happened without us having any protection than anything else.

## The Turning Point

Over the years Benetta and I continued to have marital problems. We were both very young, and we both had our own opinions of what we thought would make us happy at the time. I felt like the more I pursued things that I thought would make me happier such as golf and real estate, the more Benetta pulled in the opposite direction. Before I knew it, we had grown more and more apart. I found myself longing for what I felt like I wasn't getting in the marriage. While working in the blood lab, I began working with a white lady coworker that will remain nameless. She and I became pretty close. Rumor spread that she and I were having an affair, and the word got back to Benetta. I let things go too far with this young lady.

This young lady had been an employee at Mercy Hospital. We had worked some nights together. She eventually left the hospital to attend school at OSU. She asked me to come up for a visit. Using poor judgment, I went to the OSU campus to visit her. We attended a drive-in movie and bought some popcorn at the concession stand. I made one big mistake that night, other than the obvious—which was meeting this young lady at all. I used my credit card for payment. Back then they called to verify to see if the person using the card was that person. The concession stand lady called the house, and Benetta answered the phone. She described me and described the young lady that was accompanying me. The lady told Benetta that we were sharing popcorn at the concession stand.

Later that night we went to a party on campus, and I fell asleep after the party. I didn't get home that night until after 5:00 a.m. When I returned home, Benetta was furious! I noticed blood at the front door as soon as I got to the door. Benetta had gotten so mad that she rammed her hand through the window pane in the front door. Benetta's father took her to the ER where she received stitches. I felt really bad and apologized to Benetta. I also didn't see that young woman again after that. Benetta accepted my apology, but things were never the same. I guess the betrayal was something that she never really got over. This lady later sent me a letter in the mail, and Benetta somehow got access to it. I snatched it from her and tore it into pieces and threw it in the trash.

Later on, Benetta took the letter from the trash. I don't know how she did it, but she managed to piece it back together, and she wrote the lady back. I have no idea what she said to that lady, but I never heard from her again. I never realized the extent and damage that this placed in our marriage. Feeling betrayed by my relationship with this white woman, Benetta began to pursue more worldly things. She began wearing makeup again. She even started dressing in a more worldly manner like hot pants and shorts and halter tops and also left the church. She became what the church calls a backslider. I had to admit I wanted her to loosen up a bit, but I didn't realize that doing this would mean her leaving the church.

Not long after that, Benetta told me that she had decided to make some changes in her life, which included going to nursing school. This was something that she aspired to do while in high school, but with us starting a family, she put this off for a while. I supported her with the decision to go to nursing school. I thought this would be a very good thing for the family. I figured this would be the chance for our family to move ahead financially and begin moving toward my dream of owning rental properties.

## *Things Change*

I bought Benetta a little car so that she could get back and forth to her classes. It was a small, green-and-black Ford vehicle. Indeed, it wasn't much to look upon, but my philosophy was that as long as it was getting her from A to B, it was a good car. Bennetta thought the car was ugly. She thought that it was old. She hated the color. She hated everything about that car. I felt like Benetta was being ungrateful. How I saw it was if I didn't buy the car, then she wouldn't have had a way to get to school. Of course, she didn't see it that way at all.

Benetta toughed it out, and after two years she received her degree in nursing. I was very proud of her. I figured now that she had her degree and once she started working, we could work together and begin saving money. Eventually, we would have enough saved to invest in real estate. But Benetta completed the nursing program and became what was known back then as "a liberated woman." Benetta began thinking more independently. I felt like a lot of this was due to the women's liberation movement that was taking place across the country as well as the influence of her friends and family.

The women's liberation movement was a big thing at this time. Women Benetta's age sought to be freed from oppression and male supremacy. I guess another reason could have stemmed from her having been a stay-at-home mom for several years. For several years, she took care of the house, kids, and me. She did all the cooking and cleaning and laundry. She made sure the kids got to different places involving school, and so forth. For several years, her primary focus was on us and never really on herself.

Once Benetta got her degree, she started working and began making her own money. Then she started making more decisions on her own. She began doing more things on her own, like traveling with some of her friends. She and her hair beautician went to California together. She told me she was doing things that she wanted to do now. But she was doing them regardless of how I felt about it, and that became a problem in the marriage.

Benetta got a job working as a nurse at the VA in Dayton, Ohio. As soon as the money began coming in, she began spending money feverishly. I began wondering where her money was going. It always seemed like her bank account was empty. I encouraged her to open up an account at the VA credit union. I was hoping that we could begin to save money and hopefully soon start working on owning those properties I had always talked about.

Instead of saving money, Benetta wanted to buy a new car. She wanted to get a maid to help with the house chores and other things. I didn't understand all of these requests. I tried to block Benetta from getting a new car. She was able to get it anyhow. She purchased a sky blue-and-white 1975 Cutlass Supreme vehicle. It was custom-made at that. I thought this was a waste of money. I even gave her an ultimatum: it was either the car or the marriage, and she purchased the car anyway.

I kept insisting that we should save our money. I kept telling Benetta we needed to invest our money in real estate. This was a way for us to get ahead. But Benetta had her plans. I only wished that we had been able to get on the same page. Again, our differences were taking us in two different directions. I thought Benetta was a victim of her upbringing and could only think about the here and now. I realize now that a big part of what we were going through was because we were both very young at the time, and we both had a lot to learn.

As time went on, I thought things were getting a little better in the marriage, but to my surprise, one day Benetta said she wanted a divorce. I couldn't believe my ears. We had been together for nine years. I begged Benetta not to get a divorce and to try to work out things in the marriage, but she told me that she wanted *to be free*. Benetta and I had a heated discussion, and out of poor judgment, I slapped her. I was upset, but I did not want a divorce. I didn't realize at the time that lashing out at her was not the way to keep a divorce from happening.

I worried about how my girls would be raised. I was so angry with Benetta that I went pretty much berserk, and one evening, I tore up the house from head to toe. I took the kids to the babysitter, and I waited in that house for her to come home. But she didn't come home that night. Benetta was supposed to come home that evening, but her father told her not to go home. He knew how mad I was, and he knew I was waiting for her to get home from work. That was a very hard, very long night for me that night. Oh but for grace. Grace showed up again. She is always on time.

After I found out that Benetta would not be returning to Springfield and was staying in Dayton with her mother, Once again I became outraged. It was bad enough that she wanted a divorce, but now my kids would be at a distance from me. I knew at this point that the marriage was over. I just prayed and hoped that it would not hurt the girls. It hurt me when she moved the girls to Dayton away from me. I saw them every other weekend, but it was never like before. I had developed a bond with my girls. It took all my strength to go on with my life.

## The Custody Battle

I took Benetta to court for custody of my girls. It was a long, tedious battle, and we both fought hard to get the judge to decide in our favor. Not thinking straight, I took a gun with me to the custody hearing. I had not planned to use it, but I had decided at the moment that I was fed up with Benetta. So, I took my gun with me, and right before time to go into the building for the hearing, I sat in the car where I spent several minutes trying to figure out how to put the bullets in the gun. I must have sat there for a good fifteen minutes trying to figure it out. I never did figure it out. I ended up throwing the gun back in the car and locking it up. This was another time that I am sure that my mother was praying for me. And grace was once again standing close by.

The custody battle continued for some time. I was determined not to let go. I did not know how my girls would be living and did not want any negative outside influences in their lives. I believe at that time that we both said some things that we regret having said. It took both of us several years to see and understand where we both were at that time in our lives. The judge decided in Benetta's favor, and she was granted custody of both the girls. The rest was history. I continued living in our house on Corlington, and Benetta and the kids continued to reside in Dayton. Benetta remarried shortly after the custody battle was over.

For some time following the custody battle, I thought back on memories of times that I shared with my daughters. I thought about those things that we did together that were especially significant to me, like the times I would hold my youngest daughter in my hands and fly her in the air as she made coo, coo sounds. This was how I came up with her nickname "Cooley." And I thought about the times that I sat down at the kitchen table with my oldest, helping her with her math, drilling those numbers into her head so that she could pass her math tests and proofread her with her homework.

Those special moments dwindled to weekend visits where we sat at the kitchen table and conversed over a happy meal and a box of famous recipe chicken. The weekly visits gradually turned into every-other-weekend visits. Then there were summer visits, and they turned into every-other-summer visits. Those ultimately became "whenever" summer visits. You have a picture of your child as a child in your mind, and you keep that picture in your mind for so long, and then you look up and that child is almost an adult. Then they are adults, and before you know the years have gone by and you realize that, that time is gone and you can never get those years back.

# Chapter 12

# THE PLAY OFF

## *The City Amateur Golf Tournament*

I tried to go on with my life and to get back to normalcy as much as possible. Of course, competing in golf was a big part of my life, so that is what I continued to do. In 1980, I entered Springfield's City Amateur Championship for the third time. This event would provide a memorable finish to an otherwise bland tournament. The leader had a superior lead right from the start in this event. From the onset of the tournament, the leader posted a "super" round of golf. You would expect a player with seven previous City Amateur Championships titles to play this well.

The opening round of 68 (4 under par) put the leader well ahead of the field. After the third round, it was apparent that the rest of the golfers were playing for second place. I entered the final round well aware of several of the players who would challenge me for 2nd place. I put my mind to the task at hand. "Play your best and let the chips fall where they may," I said. "Play your best. Play the golf course, that's all you can do," and that is exactly what I did.

As the scores were displayed on the tablet sheets, the leader, as expected, won his 8th title. And then there were three golfers including me tied for second place and forcing a playoff. We all grabbed our golf clubs and headed to the first tee. We were given the rules of play of a sudden-death elimination playoff. The essence of what had been a medal play event had become a match play.

The first hole was uneventful. All players posted par 4s and moved on to the 2nd tee. The tee shots on the 2nd hole put all of us within reach of the green. I was first up, and I hit the green, leaving myself a considerable long putt of about 90 feet from the hole. Both of my competitors missed the green and were left with short chips to the hole.

Even though I was on the green, I was the farthest player away from the hole. I stepped up and studied the ninety-foot putt, thinking that if I could two putt, I may win this hole or at least eliminate one of one of the other competitors. I stroked the putt and watched the ball as it rolled slightly downhill on the true line toward the hole. The closer the ball approached the hole, the better the putt looked. The crowd all gasped with anticipation of the ball making it into the hole. I thought it had a good chance of going in. I felt my heart as it began beating louder and louder. Finally, the ball disappeared into the hole, and I let out a loud whoop and holler. You could say I yelled! Everyone knew that if my fellow competitors could not chip in from off the green, it was over.

I watched my opponents one by one as they took their shots and gave their best performance at trying to extend this playoff. All of their valiant efforts failed. As the last player's ball rolled across the green, the game was over. I was ready to celebrate another runner-up title in the Springfield City Amateur Golf Tournaments. This was one time that I was excited about and second place!

## *Goodbye Marcia*

My sister Marcia and I had been in contact with one another off and on over the years. After she graduated from Knoxville College, she developed what many might call a nomadic lifestyle. She would be in one place, and then the next thing we knew, she was somewhere else. She moved from one state to another out West. Her whereabouts were usually questionable. I was happy to find out that she had finally settled down and established a residence in Los Angeles, California. It was there that she befriended our first cousin, J.W. Hobby. From what I heard, they continued to stay in close contact with one another. We were glad to know that she had a close relative nearby.

Then one day we got some news that no one likes to hear about their loved one or a family member. We found out that Marcia was not in good health. She had been diagnosed with having uterine cancer. When Marcia became ill, she confided in J.W., and he was there to offer advice and support. He encouraged Marcia on several occasions to seek medical attention and to start some sort of treatment for the cancer. JW knew that medical science had advanced to the point that many people that had been diagnosed with this type of cancer had received treatment and survived. But Marcia had decided not to receive any medical treatment but to put the cancer in the hands of God. She said she would rather rely on prayer and her faith and that God would heal her. It wasn't too long after that that she ended contact with J.W. as well as all the other members of our family.

The family kept Marcia in their prayers and hoped for the best but feared the worst. I don't think anyone in the family disputed her having faith that God would heal her, but I think we all just wanted her to put some action with her faith by letting the doctors treat her for cancer. God can use doctors to heal a person as well. J.W. didn't hear from Marcia for some time before he began to become concerned. That's when J.W. decided to satisfy his concerns and made an unexpected visit to her home.

Once he got there, he didn't see any trace of Marcia. Her neighbors confirmed one of our worst fears. Marcia passed away, and her body had been transferred to the Los Angeles City morgue for cremation. The medical examiner had inquired about the next of kin, but when no one came forth, they made plans to move forward with the cremation. Thank God that J.W. was there. He claimed Marcia's body, and the family had her body shipped to Birmingham, Alabama, where funeral arrangements were made. She was only forty-three years old. She was the first of the eight of us siblings to be laid to rest. We loved her and still miss her very much. I will forever be grateful for the pivotal part that she played in my life. She was my connection to Ohio and my attending the medical technologist program at Mercy Hospital.

**Marcia Holloway (1940–1983)**

# Latrodectus [lăt'rə-dĕk'təs]

1. A female black widow also called Latrodectus is considered the most venomous spiders in North America. She is known for her deceptive interludes. In the heat of passion, she seduces her mate and then delights in making him her next meal.

2. In lure of her prey she hangs upside down from her web and quietly waits for her prey. Once the game has been ensnared in her sticky little web, she quickly takes her comb feet and wraps it in silk.

3. Once her prey has met its defeat, she sinks her fangs deep into its body, puncturing its frail body while injecting digestive enzymes that will eventually liquify it's remains. Once completely dissolved, it becomes an instant liquid meal, and she sucks it up. Having satisfied her appetite, the black widow makes her way back to the top of the web where she once again quietly hangs awaiting the next victim.

# Chapter 13
# LATRODECTUS

## *Moving On*

The divorce and the custody battle between me and Benetta felt like the world on my shoulders. I looked for comfort in a lady that I had known for a while. I saw her one night in a nightclub while out with a few friends. She was out on the dance floor dancing and asked a good friend of mine to introduce me to her. We danced and talked for a while. Over time, we got to know each other better, and I found out that we had many things in common. I told her that I had my real estate license, and she told me she was also interested in real estate. She also liked the idea of buying and owning properties. She agreed real estate would be a good investment. Most of all, she said she was willing to support me in this venture, which I think is what got me interested in pursuing a relationship with her.

The relationship between Charlotte and I became serious. She had three boys that she raised as a single parent. None of their fathers were in their lives. Charlotte and I eventually got married, and I became a father figure for her boys. You might say, I was the father that none of them ever had. I did for them as I had done for my daughters and helped them with schoolwork and made sure they got good grades. in school.

I would sometimes take them golfing with me and have them caddy for me from time to time. They accompanied me sometimes when I went to the rental properties and helped me with their upkeep. We made a thing of whistling while we worked.

Charlotte's mother lost her beauty salon a few years prior, so I helped her lease another shop on the south side of Springfield. It was a nice shop, located in a corner building of the shopping square center. She managed to maintain the building, and it appeared as if she had cultivated a good clientele.

## *Real Estates Reigns*

I talked Charlotte into applying for her real-estate license, and soon we both had our real estate licenses. Both of us began spending our weekends in the real estate office, performing clerical tasks like answering phone calls and speaking with people who were interested in listing properties. Our goal at that time was to expose ourselves to property owners who were in distress and needed to sell their property quickly. Once we were able to do that, the rest was easy. We made contact with homeowners who were interested in selling their homes, and we began "assuming" the mortgages on these properties for the seller. The seller would be paid equity out of the property, and we would assume the loan. This is formerly called a loan assumption deal. Over the years, we obtained full ownership of the property. As time went on, we began obtaining properties all over Springfield and putting them up for rent.

I managed the properties. My task was to maintain the property so that the property was well maintained, and it would create a high level of profit when sold. I would perform certain maintenance tasks such as painting, lawn care, other cleaning tasks, and landscaping. I also continued working the night shift as a night lab technician at Mercy Hospital. Charlotte continued to run her beauty shop and worked in real estate part-time. I thought that together we made a pretty good team and lived well. Her beauty salon became well known all over town, and she gained some notoriety for having been successful.

We moved toward our goal, and I maintained a dream of owning enough houses to sell and buying land where I could build multi unit apartment complexes. To reach this goal, I was willing to make certain sacrifices like continuing to drive my old used car that was fully paid for. As long as Charlotte and I were moving toward our goal together, I was content.

It's my opinion that Charlotte began letting her success go to her head. Over time she started spreading rumors, exaggerating about what we owned and tried to give the impression that she was doing better than she was. It was all about appearances and social status for her. She had to have on the finest clothes and expensive shoes. She had to have her nails done and have tons of makeup and hair. She leased a Nissan 300Z sports car and was driving it all around like she was hot stuff. She was a status seeker, and it was all about what it looked like on the outside for her.

The years went by as they always do, and before we knew it her oldest son was graduating from high school and going off to serve in the military. It wasn't too soon after that her next-to-oldest son graduated from high school and went off on his own. With just her youngest son being at home now, I was looking forward to us having an empty nest soon. I figured that once all the boys were grown and moved out on their own, that would allow us to do some traveling.

Even though I had a full schedule with working at the hospital and maintaining the real estate properties, I never let go of my passion for golf. I continued to get out there and practice my swings when the time would permit, and I also competed when I had the chance.

## *A one in a million shot!*

In (1986) I participated in the Bank of Ohio golf scramble. I had not planned on playing in this tournament. I was invited to play to take another player's place. Because he could not participate in this tournament, I was asked to fill in. There were approximately forty teams in a four-man team event. There were vehicles on display on all of the par 3 holes. Anyone who had a hole in one would win the vehicle on display.

Every player hit the tee shot from the par 3 hole. When my turn came up, I stepped up to the tee with confidence, squared my shoulders to the target, and hit the ball hard and high. The ball soared toward the hole and hit the green, then it rolled toward the hole. I could not imagine what would happen next. The person monitoring the golf shots let out a yell as the ball stayed on the line and disappeared in the hole. People were jumping up creating quite a commotion.

I hurried down to the green to retrieve the ball in the midst of being congratulated. For a minute, my eyes couldn't focus on anything but the Dodge Dakota pickup truck, valued at over $10,000, that was obviously to be my prize. I was told that if I accepted the prize, I would have to declare myself a pro for the next year. This would mean that for one year, I could not compete as an amateur in any event. Of course, I accepted the prize, and my amateur title was revoked. Charlotte came out to celebrate with me. She could hardly contain her joy and was quick to suggest what we should do with our windfall. Her sights were set on satisfying a lifelong dream of living in a prestigious neighborhood on the north side of town.

I posted the truck for sale and received two or three offers. I eventually sold it for $7,200 and used the money toward the downpayment on a home on the north side of Springfield. The north side of town was supposed to be where the more prestigious people in Springfield lived. When I went to look at it, I thought it was a pretty good investment. It had curb appeal. We found a tenant to rent our house on Corlington Drive and closed the real estate purchase on Derr Road.

---

## *Divorce, Part 1*

---

I thought things were going pretty well in the new home. However, about six months after moving into this new home, one day out of the blue, Charlotte came to me and said that she wanted a divorce. I didn't take her seriously at first. She was getting everything she wanted out of the marriage. Things were not perfect between us, but by no means did I see this coming. She started letting her so-called notoriety get to her head. She thought that she had achieved some social high that she had not achieved. Not all the clothes, money, or cars could make her be the person that she thought she was. We maintained our lives in the same house for a while, and then she started sleeping in one room while I slept in the other. Then she lived in one part of the house, and I lived in the other part of the house.

I later found out that she had been seeing another guy. I also found out that she told this guy and had been telling other people around town that I was a janitor. She wanted to give the people and her men friends the impression that she was earning the majority of the money in the marriage. She felt that she was the engine driving the train when she was nothing more than the caboose. It was during this time that I found out just how much of a nutcase she was. One evening while getting ready for bed, I was in my room upstairs in my bedroom, and I heard loud music coming from downstairs. I went downstairs to check it out, and I was shocked to see her. She was dancing in the middle of the living room performing the "doing the butt" dance to the song. She was also wearing a gun holster with a gun in it. It was quite the spectacle. There she was with a gun holster and gun around her waist "doing the butt flapping up and down." You picture it. I guess she thought that wearing short shorts and dancing with her butt in the air was going to entice me or tease me in some way. It only proved to show that she was crazy.

I called my attorney, and he suggested that I call the police. When the cops arrived, she was still wearing the gun holster and gun. I explained to them that we were in the middle of a domestic squabble and getting a divorce was likely. They listened to what we both had to say and left, taking her gun with them. After a few days passed, she left the house. She abandoned the house for two whole weeks, and I did not know where she was. I called a locksmith and changed the locks on the house. I took some vacation time and went to Florida to golf at one of the golf clubs. When I returned, she was in the house. I asked her why she moved back. She never did tell me why she returned, but I found out soon enough.

She persuaded her sixteen-year-old son to act as a witness against me. She accused me of threatening to kill her. My attorney was surprised that she managed to have a judge go along with her claim. With the accusation, she was able to get a restraining order against me. She felt that if I was not in the house it would be easier for her to get the house in a settlement. The restraining order was to get me out of the house.

I was escorted back to the house by officers to get my belongings. The female officer asked me why I was leaving, since I had done nothing wrong. I moved in with a cousin of mine on the other side of town. Eventually, the court decided that I should continue to collect rent and manage the properties until we had reached a divorce settlement. She would have to pay the mortgage note on the Derr Road property.

After I moved out, she moved her boyfriend into the house. This took a lot of nerve! This was a low blow, even for somebody like her. But then again, I was dealing with a low down woman, and everybody knew it. Sometime after all this took place, while at a local barbershop, I ran into Roger Evans, a former Springfield chief of police, and he made this statement: "If it was me, I would have killed both of them for living in my house before a divorce settlement was reached." Then he put forth a mischievous smile. My reply was "Roger, I know you're not serious. God will take care of this and her in time," and you can be sure that He did exactly that!

There were so many things wrong with this lady. For one, she was a pathological liar. For two, she tried to denigrate my kids, and for three, she was promiscuous. I could go on and on with the list. She had no morals whatsoever. Her girlfriend put her down for trying to seduce her boyfriend. I later found out that she was known for saying at the beauty shop that one man was not enough for her.

To top that off, during the divorce, she tried to cut my throat by threatening to report my underreporting of income to the IRS if I didn't give her the Derr Road house in the settlement. She thought that she could be considered an innocent spouse, filing an innocent spouse claim. Eventually, she did go to the IRS, and I ended up hiring a tax attorney. My attorney negotiated a settlement, and we ended up filing separate tax returns for the years that she alleged that she was making more money than we claimed.

## *The Divorce, Part 2*

The divorce took many twists and turns. I dropped claims of ownership of two-house rental properties plus released any interest in her beauty salon. But that was not enough for Charlotte; her "eyes" were in that house on Derr Road, her principal residence. She wanted me to assign the Derr Road mortgage to her. I heard some rumors that she was bragging around town about how she had beat me out of the house. Then she started making threats that she was going to turn me into the IRS, alleging that I had not reported all of her income to the IRS.

At this time we were at a stalemate. For one thing, she did not even qualify for a "new" mortgage, and I was not about to leave myself liable for the mortgage even if I signed a quit claim on the house and gave it to her. The final decision had to be made by the court. The decision was that we were to sell the house and split the net proceeds down the middle. I was shocked when her boyfriend, Edwin, made an offer to purchase the house. I balked at the thought that she would continue to reside in that house. I was being stubborn, but I also didn't want to buy her out. My thoughts were that the all-electric house was too expensive to maintain.

When presented with the Edwin offer, I refused to sign off on it. I told the attorney and the court that the offer was tainted. It was not an "arm's length" offer. The court decided to "consummate the sale." Even though the decision was made, I continued to tie it up in court. I employed another attorney to appeal the local court's decision. This would tie the house up in court for two more years. Meanwhile, Charlotte and Edwin were mandated to pay a mortgage of $659.99 per month for the mortgage.

I could have tied the case up until it reached the Supreme Court. Yet I concluded that the legal fees that I would have to pay to do that would be impractical. In pure disgust, I finally gave my attorney power-of-attorney to consummate the sale, and Mr. Edwin bought himself a house. Now, you would think that this would have been enough, but of course, it was not. In an attempt to cut my throat, she went to the IRS and alleged that she had earned more income during the time of our marriage than I had reported on our joint tax return with claims of being the innocent spouse.

I hired a tax attorney. He finalized my settlement in a negotiation that allowed us to file a separate tax return for the years in question that she claimed she had earned additional income. Her plan backfired, and she ended up owing the IRS a ridiculous amount of money in back taxes, including personal, state, and local taxes as well as Social Security taxes. Since she knew that if she held onto the two properties that I forfeited claims to, that most likely liens would be placed on them, so she sold those houses. When all the dust cleared, I retained possession of the house on Corlington Drive and four of the rental properties. It was a long winding road, but I thank God I survived.

## The Chickens Come to Roost

I tried to rid myself of all connections with Charlotte. Just when I thought that my interactions with Charlotte were over, I received a phone call from an attorney who was representing an Italian couple in a discrimination lawsuit. Charlotte was suing them, alleging that they refused to allow a showing of the parcel of land she wanted to see. I informed him that she had a problem with telling the truth. It's like the word *truth* is not in her vocabulary. I agreed to testify at the hearing, and I told them that she was a pathological liar and a very persuasive one at that. When asked to give an example of why I felt she was a liar, I told them about the rumors that she had spread in her beauty salon and that when I approached her about what she had said, she responded, "That's just n****r talk. Don't pay attention to that mess."

It took me some time to get to the truth, but sometime later, I found out that she was the "n****r" doing the talking. She tried to degrade my girls after I had helped her in raising her sons. This was only one example of how she betrayed me.

I heard many rumors over the years about Charlotte and Edwin who was now her new husband whom she saw as being her knight in shining armor. He transferred to Springfield from a trucking plant in Rock

Island, Illinois, to merge with the International Harvester trucking company. Unfortunately for him, he knew very little about Charlotte when they began their relationship. He was a conservative man, very prudent with his money. I was told that they argued about money and finances a lot, which didn't surprise me at all. Yet even with those disagreements, he seemed to be willing to try to keep her happy.

An acquaintance of mine that worked at the International Harvester credit union revealed something very interesting. Edwin had withdrawn $104,000 out of his 401K plan to serve as a downpayment on a custom-built house on the outskirts of Springfield. Once the building was complete, she threw several parties to show off the house. As usual, it was all about being seen and what it looked like, not what it was. She wanted her peers to think she had arrived. I only wondered how long it was going to last.

## The Chickens Continue to Roost

Over the years, I kept busy with my continued work as a night tech at Mercy Hospital as well as managing my real estate properties and playing a decent golf game. One day out of the blue, I received a phone call from no other than Mr. Edwin Holmes. My gut feeling when I heard his voice was that the chickens had come to roost again. He called me singing the blues. He told me all about what she had done to him and was still doing to him. I felt sorry for the dude. What made it worse was he thought that he was getting someone special.

The poor guy had just found out that Charlotte had stayed with him for ten years to get his retirement benefits. She also wanted to get some of the equity out of the custom-built house, even though she did not contribute to the down payment. *Sound familiar?* He told me he had asked around town about me and that no one had anything at all bad to say about me, but when asking about her, people always had something negative to say about her. He felt like he had awakened out of a bad dream. All I could do was wish him the best and suggested he get himself a good divorce attorney. Of course, in the end, she got as much as she could out of the man. Part of her settlement included part of his retirement income.

# Chapter 14

# A NEW BEGINNING

---

*The Golden Years*

---

I continued to live with my cousin Sadie Adams for a while. After one of my rental properties became available, I renovated it. After the renovation was complete, I decided to make this ranch style house my new place of residence. This house was not as large as the other split-level rental properties, but with me being a bachelor now, I really didn't need much space. In the year 2000, I was introduced to a lady by the name of Jacqueline McFarland through one of her close friends. Jackie and I dated for a year. We had a lot in common. Both our kids were all grown. We both liked to golf, and we were able to travel together to exotic vacation spots.

In 2001, we married at her home church of Shiloh Baptist Church in Dayton, Ohio, on March 7, 2001. We currently reside in the state of Ohio where we continue to own several rental properties that I still maintain.

---

*Retirement*

---

In 2009 I retired from Mercy Hospital after working as a staff medical technologist for over forty-seven years. I left with a full pension from the hospital and full Social Security benefits. I celebrated my retirement with the staff and was reunited with a lot of my former coworkers on this occasion. I also retired my real estate license the same year.

## *Mercy Hospital*

Mercy Hospital and Community Hospital merged in the year 2015 and are now called Springfield Regional Hospital.

## *The Final Call*

I competed in my last golf competition in 2008 where my team, representing Mercy Hospital in a prestigious charity fundraiser event sponsored by the United Way, won first place. Today I play in my spare time with the senior golfers. We call ourselves *"The Geritol Group."*

## *The Legacy*

Morris celebrates a history of golf tournament and event winnings

He's won three runner-up titles in the Springfield City amateur Golf Tournaments, and placed second in the years 1970, 1973, and 1980. He competed in the Springfield Championship League Competition (1970–1971) where he won two competitions in a row, and he was named the most improved golfer of the year by the league in 1970.

(1974) He competed in the Clark County Match Play Tournament (runner up), 2nd place.

(1976) He competed in the Clark County Match Play Tournament, 3rd place.

(1976) He competed and won the Mercy Hospital Championship Tournament.

(1977) He competed and won in the Jim Foreman Classic Tournament at Snyder Park Golf Club (Posting par golf of 144 for two days of play).

Between 1970 and 1975, he competed in both the Reid Park Golf Club Championship and the Snyder Park Golf Club Championship events and took 2nd place in both events.

(1975) He competed in the Ohio State Public Golfers Tournament (posted an opening round of 66 (6 under par).

(1976) He competed in the Cleveland Ohio State Public Golfers Tournament and posted the first recorded hole-in-one at Highland Park Golf Course in Cleveland, Ohio.

Between 1970 and 1980, he was the winner of multiple Turf Club Championship Titles

(1986) He competed in the Banc of Ohio Golf Tournament, a team event, posting a hole-in-one and winning a 1986 Dodge Dakota pickup truck valued at $10,200 dollars.

# IN LOVING MEMORY OF

*Square Morris Holloway Sr. (1875–1962)*
My dad continued to drive for Jitney Cab for several years. Then he started having circulation problems in his legs. The doctors discovered that he had a blocked artery. They tried to open the blockage, but the obstruction was too long and too hard, and there was no hope of saving his leg. A few months after the first amputation, they found out that there was some nerve and blood vessel damage in his other leg. Losing both legs was too much for him, and he gave up the fight. Not many months after his second amputation, he passed away. Square Morris Holloway Sr. passed away at age eighty-seven.

*Chanie Holloway (1915–2007)*
My mother raised up two missions and one church which she pastored, Greater Restored Kingdom of God, in 1968. She traveled over the US and Canada, doing evangelistic work for the Lord and preaching the gospel. She never stopped praying for all eight of her children and lived to celebrate a lot of their successes. She lived clear up to the ripe age of ninety-one. Overseer Chanie Holloway went home to be with the Lord on February 9, 2007.

*Marcia Holloway (1940–1983)*
My sister Marcia J. Campbell passed away at the age forty-three from uterine cancer.

*Delotha Holloway (1937–2011)*
My sister Minister Delotha Rogers passed away at age seventy-four of pancreatic cancer.

# SIBLINGS

Three of my siblings Freddie Holloway, Pastor Reginald Holloway, and Pastor Sherry Wilder still reside in the state of Alabama. My oldest sister, Minister La Grieta Miller, resides in the DC area. My sister Pastor Patricia Wapples currently lives in Atlanta, Georgia.

Square Morris Holloway Sr. and wife Chanie Holloway

# WHERE ARE THEY NOW?

## Daughters

My oldest daughter earned a Bachelor of Science in Accounting and works as a senior budget officer. My youngest daughter is a (CESP) Job Developer. She earned an associate degree, and is an author, motivational speaker, and pastor. They both reside in the state of Ohio.

## Edith Cassidy

Edith Cassidy passed away in 1983. I will never forget her friendship. She was a Godsend to me.

## Dr. Hunter

Dr Hunter passed away around the year 1982.

## Kathy Kolinos

Kathy Kolinos retired from Mercy Hospital. After her retirement, she continued to work as an instructor at the Clerk Tech Community College. With much effort she befriended me and asked me to speak to one of her classes on being a tech at the hospital. I finally accepted.

## The Carters

I remained friends with the Carters for many years. Today Mrs. Carter is around ninety-two years old, and Mr. Bill Carter died at age ninety-two. The words "Never give up" continue to resonate within me, even still today.

## First Wife, Benetta

Benetta and I did not speak to one another for over ten years. Eventually, we were able to forgive one another and began speaking to each other again. We both divorced, and we both remarried. Today we are good friends. Benetta went on to obtain her Bachelor of Science Degree in nursing in the year 1990. She worked as an evening nursing supervisor sixteen years and retired from nursing at the VA Medical Center after thirty-one years. Today she is an instructor and provides testing to STNA Students. Benetta returned back to the Church of God in Christ in the year 2000. She has obtained multiple degrees in the ministry, including her most recent: Doctorate in Philosophy in Theology. She now serves as an Evangelistic Missionary.

## *Ex Wife, Charlotte*

In the finalization of Charlotte and Edwin's divorce, Edwin sold the house, left Springfield, and returned to his hometown, Rock Island, Illinois.

### *Another Bite!*

A few years after her divorce from Edwin, Charlotte remarried to a ninety-year-old man, a former Springfield postmaster and real estate broker. He suffered from severe health problems. This marriage lasted for about a year due to his passing. After his death, there was the usual squabble over his estate. She was granted a small settlement. She rightfully earned the title for being one of the most infamous *"Gold Diggers"* that Springfield had ever produced! A year later, it has been said that she moved to Georgia, where no one has heard from her since.

## *The Future*

Out of a total of seven grandchildren and six great grandchildren, as well as the children, grandchildren, and great-grandchildren I inherited by marriage with my wife Jackie, you would think that there would be at least one competitive golfer in the bunch. Well, only time will tell. Until then...

I will reflect back and tell of the first time that I saw a little boy who could not have been more than three or four years old holding a golf club in his hand in the midst of swinging. Not only I, but many others in the golf world knew something was brewing.

# Conclusion
# ALONG CAME A TIGER

## *A Game Changer*

Tiger began making noise in the golf world at a very early age. The first time I set my eyes on Tiger, he couldn't have been more than around two or three years of age. He was on the *Michael Douglas Show,* swinging a golf club. It was amazing to see a kid swinging a golf club at that early age. So, the golf world knew that Tiger was coming, long before he arrived. His father was well known to the golf world. We knew that he was a retired Marine who cussed like a sailor. It was Tiger's father Earl who gave his son the nickname "Tiger."

It was Tiger's father Earl who put a golf club in his hand at that early age, and that's how Tiger was introduced to the game of golf. Earl would pick Tiger up and stand him in his hand, and Tiger would not lose his balance. Earl was a smart man; he knew that golf was a game of balance and that with Tiger's sense of balance, he figured he would teach Tiger how to swing a golf club at an early age.

His concentration in the game was one of a kind. While Tiger would be practicing his swing, his father Earl would do things to try to distract him in his swing. It was fascinating. Tiger would never lose focus. Tiger developed a keen sense of concentration. With Tiger's combination of balance and concentration, Earl knew that there would be no stopping him. He predicted that Tiger would change the game of golf forever—and he was right!

By the time Tiger came on the scene, the doors had already been opened and a path well paved for his arrival. Though he still had his demons to face on and off the court when it came to racism. In 1994 Tiger Woods won his first three straight US amateur titles. In 1996, he won the NCAA Division 1-A individual title as a member of the Stanford golf team. He turned professional and tied for 60th place in his debut at the Greater Milwaukee Open. From there he went on to win two PGA Tour events and was named America Player of the Year and PGA Tour Player of the Year, ranking the No. 1 spot in the world.

It was at this point in his career that many began to refer to him in ways like "the coming of Moses." He was definitely shaking up the golf world with his powerful swing and deadly putting stroke. Everyone knew that it was just a matter of time before Tiger became a well-known phenomenon.

In 1997, Tiger Woods became the first African American as well as the youngest player to win the Masters and continued to break many records in the game of golf. Over the years he has had to face many challenges and yet he remains second only to Jack Nicklaus of Columbus, Ohio, in major titles. It's been recorded that as of 2020, he is pursuing breaking Sam Snead's all-time record of PGA tournament wins.

# BIBLIOGRAPHY

*Birmingham Public Accommodation Segregation Laws. "Birmingham Public Accommodation Segregation Laws." Civil Rights Movement Archive Example Segregation Laws, Webspinner, https://www. crmvet.org/info/seglaws.htm. Accessed 25 10 2020.*

*Britannica. "Martin Luther King Jr." Martin Luther King Jr., Encyclopedia Britannica, 27 07 2020, Retrieved October 2020 from https://www.britannica.com/biography/Martin-Luther-King-Jr. Accessed 25 10 2020.*

*History. "Freedom Rides." History, A & E Television Network, 10 2 2010, https://www.history.com/topics/black-history/freedom-rides. Accessed 25 10 2020.*

*History. "Greensboro sit-in." History, A & E Television Network, 4 2 2010, https://www.history.com/topics/black-history/the-greensboro-sit-in. Accessed 25 10 2020.*

*History. "Little Rock Nine." History, A & E Television Networks, 29 01 2010, https://www.history.com/topics/black-history/central-high-school-integration. Accessed 25 10 2020.*

*Southern Company. "Paying Tribute to Black pioneers." New Center Stories, Southern Company, 18 2 2019, https://www.southerncompany.com/newsroom/2019/feb-2019/paying-tribute-to-black-golf-pioneers.html. Accessed 24 10 2020.*

*U.S Embassy & Consulate in the republic of Korea. "Sunday Bloody Sunday." U.S Embassy & Consulate in the republic of Korea,*

*U.S Consulate, https://kr.usembassy.gov/education-culture/kids/ take-trip-american-history/modern-era-1946-present/sunday-bloody-sunday/. Accessed 25 10 2020.*

*Wikipedia contributors. "American Civil War." Wikipedia, The Free Encyclopedia. Wikipedia, The Free Encyclopedia, 23 Oct. 2020. Web. 25 Oct. 2020.*

*Wikipedia contributors. "Jim Crow laws." Wikipedia, The Free Encyclopedia. Wikipedia, The Free Encyclopedia, 21 Oct. 2020. Web. 25 Oct. 2020.*

*Wikipedia contributors. "Southern United States." Wikipedia, The Free Encyclopedia. Wikipedia, The Free Encyclopedia, 23 Oct. 2020. Web. 25 Oct. 2020.*

*Wikipedia contributors. "Great Migration (African American)." Wikipedia, The Free Encyclopedia. Wikipedia, The Free Encyclopedia, 21 Oct. 2020. Web. 25 Oct. 2020.*

*Wikipedia contributors. "Tiger Woods." Wikipedia, The Free Encyclopedia. Wikipedia, The Free Encyclopedia, 19 Oct. 2020. Web. 25 Oct. 2020.*

*Wildermuth, Gene, editor. On The Putting Green with Gene Wildermuth. Springfield, Springfield News-Sun Sports, 1972.*

*"World Golf Hall Of Fame." 2020. World Golf Hall of Fame, http:// www.worldgolfhalloffame.org/. Accessed 25 10 2020.*

# ABOUT THE AUTHOR

**M**orine Slayton-Nixon, author and motivational speaker, published *Woman Where Are You?* in 2006, *"Here and Now"* in 2014, and *Exchanging a Cross for a Crown* in 2017.

**Morine is an *inspirational writer.*** She continues to inspire her readers by sharing life journeys, experiences, and God interventions. She is the founder of Crown productions, formerly known as In Christ Ministries, a book ministry. She received an Associate Degree in (1990). She began ministering as an inspiring evangelist in 2001. She attended Bible college in 2004.

**Morine:** I believe everybody has a story to tell. That story might be one's Christian testimony, life experiences, and lessons learned, or a variety of other things that have catapulted us through on this life's journey. Stories can be very powerful and leave a lasting imprint in a person's life. Sometimes stories help people see things in a clearer fashion. I believe that when we hear stories or have experiences in life that have a positive effect on us in some way, we should share those stories with others so that they too may be helped.

Contact Information:
Mailing Address:

Crown Productions
P.O Box 683
Canal Winchester, OH 43110

| Website: | www.CrownProduction.Online |
|---|---|
| Facebook: | https://www.facebook.com/mslaytonnixon |
| Email: | MSlayton-Nixon@CrownProductions.Online |

To inquire about booking Morine Slayton-Nixon for a speaking engagement, please send email to: MSlayton-nixon@CrownProductions.Online

# ALSO BY
# MORINE SLAYTON-NIXON

*Woman Where Are You?*
Morine shares her experience of moving to a new city as a new single parent and the challenges she faced along the way. This meant leaving a job, house, family church, and a list of other things. The Lord understood everything she was going through, even when no one else could. He let her know that everything was going to be okay. The transition in life sends her through times of the past as she searches for a new place in life. This is where she finds new hope on a new journey with the Lord.

*Here and Now*
Morine shares her journey and how God's faithfulness helped her to persevere through the years. She moves to inspire people of faith to awaken their dreams of the past as she awakens hers and stirs up the gifts from within. It's time to move beyond the pains of the past. It's time to plan for the future and walk into your victory!

*Exchanging a Cross for a Crown*
Morine shares her journey in this book that is full of God's inspired Word, motivational stories, and eye-opening dramatizations of where some Christians find themselves as they travel on life's journey today.

Books Available at Amazon, Barnes & Nobles.com
Xulon Press Online Book Store Page

*Morine S-N*
Crown Productions

# NOT FORGOTTEN

CPSIA information can be obtained
at www.ICGtesting.com
Printed in the USA
BVHW041501050821
613736BV00004B/41